SAMANT

The Prayer of A Single Mom

Inspired and Guided by the Lord
Our Savior and the Holy Spirit

The Prayer of the Single Mom by Samantha Gustafson
Copyright © 2015 by Samantha Gustafson
All Rights Reserved.
ISBN: 978-1-59755-380-3
Published by: ADVANTAGE BOOKS™ Longwood, Florida, USA
www.advbookstore.com

Library of Congress Catalog Number: 2015959446

First Printing: January 2016
16 17 18 19 20 21 22   10 9 8 7 6 5 4 3 2 1
Printed in the United States of America

Introduction

A tough day, a tough week, a tough year, or a tough minute, they are all the same. The same struggle every mom has ever been through on any given day. Trying to get kids to school, get to work, get a shower or even just go to the bathroom alone. Ever have those moments where you want to be alone and beg for them but when you are actually and finally alone you cry hoping for that moment to be over? And then you are left swimming in the guilt of all the moments you weren't alone. I have all of these moment, breakdowns or rollercoaster's of emotions daily if not hourly and the word crazy comes into my head. Maybe I am crazy, maybe every other mom can do this but me and then I cry some more...and then I pray.

I pray because I have absolute faith that God has put me in that moment for a reason. I pray because He has the equipment to help me through that moment and yet most importantly I pray because I know I'm not alone.

Samantha Gustafson

Table of Contents

Samantha Gustafson

Chapter 1

Single Mom's Club

I don't think many people ask to be in the Single Mom's Club. Don't get me wrong, there may be someone out there that wants to go it alone and made that choice but regardless it isn't easy. It doesn't really matter how you were initiated into the club once you are in; it is surviving that becomes the goal. Personally, I had it all. I married my hardworking, blonde haired, blue-eyed farmer high school sweetheart who happened to be my best friend and personal miracle from God. We had a beautiful home, great farm and amazing family. Add to that, as if it could get any better were two beautifully healthy sons and the white picket fence.

Brett and I met on the school bus my freshman year in high school. I was the new freshman girl with a troubled past and a hopeful future, looking for love and a place to feel at home. Brett was the quiet, oh so cute sophomore with built in confidence, a heart of gold and the family from heaven. Our eyes met the first moment I stepped on the bus and it was NOT love at first sight for him at least. I fell madly in love with him and fought the whole year to get his attention. Finally at the end of the school year on June 21 he asked me to be his girlfriend. We traveled through every part of growing up together: first cars, graduations, college for me, farm life for him and grew from a teenage couple into married adults with the world at our fingertips and a love so strong it seemed unbreakable. I share all this because it is important to my induction into the single moms club. Our whole world changed that Friday in June of 2013. We had visited Disney in January (which was one of my dreams come true to share those moments with our children) and Brett noticed a lump on his chest. It was very tiny, almost like a small white mole but it hadn't been there before. As the months grew on it started to get bigger, not by much but bigger none the less, after much nagging on my part he finally decided to see his doctor in late April and they scheduled it to be biopsied in the first week in June, a week I will never forget.

The doctor called, diagnosis given and the world crumbled at our feet. My perfectly healthy, vibrant, hardworking husband and father to our two beautiful children (then ages 3 and 1) were diagnosed with stage 4 Melanoma Skin cancer. Brett fought with everything he had, we prayed with everything we had and still, I lost him almost exactly 6 months later on December 23, 2013, two days before Christmas. There is so much more to my story, to our story and honestly I could write for days sharing the heartache of watching my partner, whom we promised to love, honor and cherish for the rest of our days, slip away from me. To watch him want to give up on a life he cherished more than anything in this world. I could rip hearts out with describing our last moments together before he took his last breath or the brief moment he came out of his seizures to wrap a pillow case around me and draw his family in close to tell them to take care of me. But as I think about sharing those moments I take a step back and reflect on what those moments did to me, how they impacted and scarred me forever. As I reflect on my pain, my anguish, my loss, my grief, I am almost always immediately hit with the sobering fact that I am not alone.

Every single parent or parent of any kind for that matter knows that you don't have time to dwell in your own emotions, feelings, fears or anxieties because your kids are more important and THEY need you. If you don't instinctively know this, the world will do a great job of enlightening you. About 15 minutes after I watched the love of my life take his last breath and leave me forever on this Earth the decisions had to be made. Which funeral home? What time can you be there tomorrow? Where do you want to be buried? On Christmas Eve, services were planned, and a burial plot chosen and then I went home to our 4 and 2 year olds and prepared for Santa's arrival. Needless to say the induction into the club is never easy and as a woman of God with more questions than answers, I am called to trust in the Lord and rely on his plan to unfold in my life.

That is a difficult take when the kids are tired, dishes are piled to the ceiling, soccer practice is tomorrow and you can't find the one sock you need to complete the uniform. Is anyone else having that bell ringing moment right now? We all know I can add so many more demands to that list. I am with you in those moments when you wish for one second you could turn to your child/children and say, "go ask daddy" or "go ask mommy." "Honey can you please watch the kids so I can pee alone?" "Bud, Daddy said no, so I say no." "Honey, I'm not feeling well can you take care of dinner tonight?" So many emotions flood through me like a mighty river when I think about all these moments. The first and the most obvious feeling, God gave us two parents for a reason! The second feeling I have is it isn't fair that I have to be the disciplinarian on my own while everyone else gets to be the "nice guys" to my kids. And the third emotion that comes through is exhaustion. Exhaustion radiates through me like an electric current to a live wire. I'm exhausted because I am grieving, I am exhausted because I am a single parent, but most importantly I am exhausted because I am a human being and our emotions can rob us of our energy.

This is when I usually hit my breakdown. Either I get a little snappier with one of my kids or I fail to complete task that I think all "good moms" should do. I begin to sink into that low of low called rock bottom. Let me just say, I have everlasting faith in the Lord through all of this, but trials are a part of life and our faith and trust in the Lord's love for use gives us the strength to preserver. At least that is my opinion.

So, I've hit that previously mentioned rock bottom and the kids are finally in bed after 2 bedtime stories, 18 thousand kisses, 15 tuck back ins, 4 sips of water and one grumpy tired mom crying uncontrollably at the bottom of the shower. Ever been there? Where for one split second you doubt, for one split second you're all alone in this pool of hopelessness, (aka, you shower with snot running down your face) and no one will ever understand or can help because they will either judge you or laugh at the insignificance of your "problems?" I UNDERSTAND!! And that is when I pray.

As I've grown closer to God, I realize that praying isn't an insignificant gesture for our own good that goes unheard. God does hear our prayers and He is the only one equipped to help for the long term. And I don't know about you, but I don't have time for a "band aid" cure. No offense to the Band Aid brand, they are getting better and can last weeks! But hey, I need a cure for these struggles in life and a wet and soggy band-aid that can last for weeks isn't cutting it. I'm sure you all know what I am talking about, you know when you become a single parent or not and life gets overwhelming there are band-aids out there. A nigh out with the girls, a bubble bath, going on a date, a glass of wine, a new project, a mini vacation, or even redecorating. If you are anything like me you have tried them all and while band-aids are great to help stop the bleeding, they don't cure the injury. And here I am again, I have used all of my band aids, I felt better for a minute and here I am, right back at the bottom of my shower, or in the middle of the kitchen floor cleaning up the 3rd spilled milk that night begging for the cure! Well I found it, GOD!

I know we've heard it all before, "believe in God and all your worries disappear." I am NOT going to tell you that, nor am I am going to pretend that I know my Bible front and back. But what I can say is that God is my personal Savior and without him I'd be a whole lot worse than sitting on the bottom of the shower a few minutes every couple of weeks. I don't pretend to have it all figured out but I do know I am not alone.

Keep your lives free from the love of money and be content with what you have, because God has said "Never will I leave you; never will I forsake you." Hebrews 13:5

I don't know about you, but those words from our Holy Bible could never be more comforting. How many of us in this club have been left? And let me be clear this isn't just about the "single mom's club" anymore, this is the club of hurting people in life.

How many of us have been left? Left by a spouse for another person? Left by addiction? Left by an accident? Left by an unforeseen event or war? Left by health struggles? Maybe you haven't even been physically left at all but emotionally. Sometimes we can have the person we love with us at all times and still feel alone and… left. I had been left and felt alone by people long before I met Brett on that school bus or became a mom. But it comforts me knowing that I will NEVER be alone again. Some people ask me how do I know GOD is real. If God is real why are bad things happening?

1. I don't know all that God knows and NEVER will I try to speculate.

2. MY proof is people; as many people that are out there making bad choices there are so many that are doing good. It happens when you finally open your eyes to see the little goodness sprinkled all around you. The smile from a stranger, the community that comes together to help the fire victims from down the street to the person that bought your coffee because you looked like you were having a rough morning. THESE are God's works from his people and my goodness I really want to be a part of that.

3. Most importantly: ***"Suffer hardship with me, as a good solider or Christ Jesus*** -2 Timothy 2:3

God never promised our life to be easy and lined with gold and riches but He did promise to give us everything we need to do His will. So as I end my sob fest at the bottom of the shower and my rollercoaster of emotions has pulled into the station it always ends on blessed.

And then I pray.

"Lord, please help me to be the person you designed and created me to be. I know you have me exactly where I need to be and I trust your plan. But please give me strength to follow your path and surround me with your love so I can carry that love, patience and forgiveness you give to me onto my children. In Jesus great name, Amen."

Chapter 2

My Struggles…
Is anyone out there?
Can I get an Amen?

We all have struggles and I am not EVER going to pretend for one second that mine are any more difficult than yours. Maybe the point of this book, of interaction, of communication, of fellowship and even of mankind is for us to realize we aren't that much different. Sure, lifestyles, clothes, location, socio economic status and even race can distinguish us from one another but aren't we all still women, people, mothers? Young, old, black, white, rich, poor, single, married, educated, uneducated, children or no children, WE STRUGGLE! Inherently and surprisingly if you take 5 minutes to listen to a neighbor or the lady in front of you at the grocery store you'd realize you aren't that much different!

I am a self-reflective person, aka a woman. I look at every situation a million ways and beat it to death until I find a solution; I am willing to bet that I am the only woman in the world like that right? If you are shaking your head right now and picturing all the situations you try to fix and control then perhaps I am not alone!

Being a single mom is only part of my identity. I am also an independent Christian woman with thoughts, thoughts that go well beyond potty training and bedtimes. In my life or should I say in this season, being a single mom does greatly shape my thoughts and feelings. The feeling that plagues my every thought (well maybe not my every thought but most of them), the answer to the million-dollar question: what is the most negative feeling you have about yourself on a regular basis is inadequacy.

I know, I know, SHOCKER, right? No mom should ever feel inadequate or not good enough because we are superwomen right? Even if you are not a mom; women are strong, powerful and determined. They can run fortune 500 companies, carpool, organize school dances, pack lunches, head up any afterschool club or sport, work 50+ hours a week and still manage to shower (most of the time) and have meaningful relationships with spouses, children or friends. So how, if we are capable of all of this plus the millions of other things we all do on a regular basis how is there room for inadequacy?

Maybe I am the only one out there that feels inadequate. But for some reason I feel if I took a poll of 50 women (and this is NOT based on fact) and asked them if they often felt inadequate or not good enough on a regular basis I bet 49 would say yes (and the last one was fibbing)! If you have never felt this then please pray for me and send me your secret. But in all seriousness, I struggle with inadequacy as a mom, as a woman, I used to as a wife and as a Christian.

As a mom thoughts came like, "Did I play with them enough?" "Did I listen to their thoughts and feelings?" "Do they know I love them?" "Did I cook good enough meals?" "Were the meals healthy enough?" "Am I strict enough?" "Am I flexible enough?" The list could be never ending. As a woman, "Am I working hard enough?" "Am I dressed appropriately?" As a wife, "Am I skinny enough?" "Do I show my love enough?" "Do I cook enough meals?" "Do we make love enough?" "Am I sexy enough?" And as a Christian, "Do I help enough people?" "Am I faithful enough?" "Do I tithe enough?" "Am I witnessing enough?" The list and inadequacies could go on for miles. Now after reading that I hope that your thought isn't, "oh she's nuts, I'm not THAT crazy?" My response is: I hope other people don't share my level of struggles with inadequacy but if you do its okay!

I have to dare to say that if we are honest with ourselves, we have all felt one of more of these on several occasions throughout the season of our lives. However, my problems aren't recognizing my feelings (I'm obviously pretty good at that), it's how to deal with these feelings through Christ, and so I am not "band aiding." I say this because the following was how I was or how I have seen others deal with their same feelings of inadequacies.

Band Aid to Women Inadequacy Issues

1. Tear down other women/mothers to make yourself feel less inadequate (bet you have never used or seen this band aid used).

2. Join a support group: aka, you best friend answering the phone at 2 am listening to you crying from your bathtub about how you've never been good enough and never will be.

3. Drown out those thoughts by taking on 15 more projects to prove you aren't inadequate.

4. You start talking to yourself and giving yourself praise every time you have a good moment. You did it, Samantha, you got all the laundry done, lunches packed, worked all day, made dinner, played with the kids, bath, book and bed. You deserve a medal. I defiantly haven't done this…

Ok, so I am not going to tell you which of these are me but I'd be willing to bet we have some personal experience with one or more; either doing it our self or seeing it happen. My guess is that none of these has fixed the feelings of inadequacies but they have sure made you feel good for a short minute, aka a band-aid!

Now that I am growing closer to Christ, I know I can do all things through Christ, so why can't tackling my negative self-feelings be one of those things? I guess the answer lies in the question. Because I have negative self-worth! Don't ask me where it comes from; maybe society (we like to use that a lot), maybe childhood (that is a good one too) or maybe it's an actual lack of faith. I started questioning my faith on top of all my questions about myself. How can I not love myself and think I'm a good enough mom, wife, woman or Christian when God, our creator loves me so much? My answer every time is I am not worthy of that kind of love.

John 3:16 says: ***"For God so loved the world, that He gave his only son, that whoever believes in him should not perish but have eternal life."***

That scripture leaves me in awe every time. I know the love I have for my sons and I couldn't imagine loving someone else (especially someone imperfect) that I would sacrifice my son for them. These are the moments I have trouble-letting God in to help me with my human inadequacy because I feel unworthy of a love that great. Anyone ever feel that way? I mean honestly, sometimes I feel unworthy of human love let alone God's unwavering love. That's when it happened, I confessed my feelings of inadequacy to the ladies at my Bible study and we talked through it. And one of my friends, Cindy, spoke up and said "but you aren't worthy, it is through Grace that you receive His love."

Grace; one simple word, one that has forever changed my perspective on my inadequacies, and my lack of worthiness for God's unfailing love, and grace. We aren't worthy of His love and He doesn't ask us to be perfect. He loves us just the way we are. He has always loved us and not for whom we can be but for whom we are. It took a little digging and praying but right there in my Bible, I yet again found the answer I was seeking, the peace I needed to calm my constant feelings of inadequacies.

"But God, being rich in mercy, because of the great love with which He loved us, even when we were dead in our trespasses, made us alive together with Christ- by grace you have been saved". Ephesians 2: 4-5

I know now that I can stop fighting the battle within myself of whether I am worthy or adequate. I guess the question would be adequate for whom? God loves me and you just the way we are. Sure, He has expectations for us once we come to Him to be saved but all of those expectations are for our safety and His glory. I guess now knowing that through grace I am redeemed and worthy in His eyes, practicing and doing come next. Yup, you guessed it; I found a scripture for that too. Sometimes, even as I write I wonder how anyone or I can ever doubt God and His love for us. At the exact moment of writing this I was led to yet another amazing scripture.

"Humble yourselves, therefore, under the mighty hand of God so that at the proper time He may exalt you, casting all you anxieties on him because He cares for you." Peter 5: 6-7

Every day is still a struggle. Like I mentioned in the previous chapter, I don't think our struggles magically disappear, but what I do think is that Christ helps us through them and with struggle comes strength and purpose. Can we survive the everyday struggle to succeed to our purpose? I'd like to hope and pray for strength to succeed. And I leave my inadequacies with this.

"But you, O Lord, are a God merciful and gracious, slow to anger and abounding in steadfast love and faithfulness." Psalms 86:15

And then I pray:

"Lord, I thank you always for all the blessings you bestow on me. The ones I recognize and the ones I have yet to understand. God, please help me in my struggle to love myself in the way you love me. Please help me to always remain confident yet humble in my life to bestow any glory you give me straight to you God because I am nothing without you. I

thank you always for your grace, love and forgiveness and pray your will on my life because your love is enough. In Jesus' great name I pray. Amen"

Chapter 3

Mary or Martha?

"As Jesus and his disciples were on their way, He came to a village where a woman named Martha opened her home to him. She had a sister called Mary, who sat at the Lord's feet listening to what He said. But Martha was distracted by all the preparations that had to be made. She came to him and asked, "Lord, Don't you care that my sister has left me to do the work by myself? Tell her to help me." "Martha, Martha," the Lord answered, "You are worried and upset about many things, but few things are needed or in deed only one. Mary has chosen what is better, and it will not be taken away from her." Luke 10: 38-42

All I could say after reading this story is, wow! How many of us are Martha? And how was Martha to know that what she was doing was less important than the task Mary was doing, which was listening. It seems from this text, even in biblical times women found the need to be hostesses. I don't know about you, but my need to be the best Martha I can be feeds my inadequacy beast. If you are anything like me, the tendency to dwell on the things to do is almost all consuming. For the most part I do believe that society plays a huge role in our to do list and the anxiety that inevitably follows, but what is there to do?

For some reason I feel completely unequipped to dig into or interpret this story. However, I find the need to not beat myself up. As I've listened to sermons based on this scripture it seems so many people have varying opinions ranging from let everything else go but Christ, to the perspective that only Martha's final attitude towards her sister's lack of help came to be the problem. Jesus never reprimanded or scolded Martha for her efforts of hosting. In fact, He never scolded her at all. He simply responded to her request and feelings. The more I think about this scripture the more I wonder if Martha's actions were necessarily the problem. She was working hard to please the Lord, she wanted to honor His presence and show how much she loved and appreciated Him. So why then do we read this scripture and feel bad about ourselves and our busy lives?

We always feel like it's our need to be the perfect woman, with the perfect home, perfect kids, perfect family or the perfect job. I feel like we feel this way because deep down we know that God should always come first and this story reminds us of that point, and Jesus said so himself. Does it always have to be one way or another? Can we give our lives and love to the Lord fully and still maintain our responsibilities for our Martha lives? I believe we can!

Instead of constantly beating myself up and falling back into the trap of feeling inadequate, I choose to dig further into scripture for guidance and peace.

> *"Do not neglect to show hospitality to strangers, for by doing this some have entertained angels without knowing it."* Hebrews 13:2

> *"Contributing to the needs of the saints, practicing hospitality."* Romans 12:13

> *"She watches over the affairs of her household and does not eat the bread of idleness. Her children arise and call her blessed; her husband also, and He praises her: "many women do noble things, but you surpass them all."* Proverbs 31: 27-29

The Holy Bible, our words of encouragement and guidance left by our creator to help us in these most difficult of moments and struggles in life honors the work of a woman, "(She) does not eat the bread of idleness" (Proverbs 31:27). There are always times that we need to be restful and reflective in our lives but I don't feel as though the story of Mary and Martha teaches us that. I feel as though the Lord is teaching us it's ok to be Martha, but to be aware of priorities and the Lord should always come first.

Let's face it, He is the reason we have those beautiful children to raise, however crazy they drive us, the home we need to clean, the clothes we need to wash, the job that stresses us out, and all the other things on our list. Yet through prayer, praise, thanks and hope from the Lord we can be Martha with a thankful Mary soul.

And then pray:

"Lord I come to you in thanks. Thank you for all the blessings you give me daily, all the blessings I recognize and especially those I don't. Please open my eyes and heart to continue my Martha work ethic while building my Mary soul. I want to see all the work you are doing in my life and recognize when it times to slow down for you. I give you all the honor, glory and praise, in Jesus' name. Amen"

Chapter 4

How Do We Do This?

Isn't that a million dollar question for you? Honestly, I can't tell you, so maybe I'm not qualified to write this book, or give you my opinion. Maybe that is what the enemy wants us to think and feel, unqualified, unprepared, inadequate and hopeless. Isn't that the way the serpent made Eve feel? She was confident, strong and happy and he talked her into feeling less than adequate, unknowledgeable and lacking. It was on these feelings that the first sin against God was committed. These feelings led Eve to question, which in turn into questioning, then doubt and doubt spawned sin. Now that I say that phrase aloud and think it in my head, I know this is even a daily if not hourly struggle for me. So how do we do this? How do we fight the enemy? How do we fight the feelings of inadequacy and doubt, so we don't fall into the same trap all those who came before us have fallen into? We pray, we hope, we read, and we build strength in the love of our Savior and creator. Is that easy? NO! So I dedicate this chapter to hope filled scriptures that we can hang on to in those moments of weakness, fear, anger, anxiety, loss, despair, and doubt.

Before I begin the word of the Lord, I must share how the Lord led me here. I am not a professional author, but I am a flawed, yet obedient servant of God. When you pray about your future, your hopes and dreams and you pray for God to use you and his answer is write a book. Well, then I guess you write a book. I love to write and always have. Reading and writing have been two of my favorite past times for years because for a brief moment they allow you to escape. God had my story already written from the time I was created in my mother's womb. He knew what my struggles would be but more important what my victories could be (with my cooperation of course). So it didn't surprise me when the Lord had me begin to write this book. However, the content to which I was to write has been a surprise. You are literally a part of my journey with the Lord. You are reading a reflection of my obedience to Him and even a reflection of my flaws and stubbornness. But part of writing this book is to share just how amazing and patient our God is.

The time is literally 1:29 AM. What would I rather be doing right now? That's right you called it… sleeping! It's a rainy February, well I guess its morning now, I can hear the rain on the roof outside (perfect sleeping conditions), and all my kids are in bed and haven't gotten out of bed since I tucked them in, which is in and of its self a miracle from God himself! So why am I awake? The answer; because our God is amazing and He is patient and kind. As I mentioned before I am a human being, flawed, emotional, tired, overwhelmed and impatient at times. When God gave me the idea for this book months ago, He laid out the table of contents for me, right there in clear detail as if I had written it myself. The content inside those chapters has been coming little by little. When I set out to start this chapter I prayed and prayed. I knew He gave me the title for the chapter but as you could probably tell in my intro I felt completely unequipped to give advice on how to do this when I wasn't even sure I could myself. Almost as soon as I said those words out loud, it hit me like a ton of bricks, "I can't do it myself!" When in doubt, when in fear or times of struggle where do I turn? To the word of God I can always count on, thus leading me to this chapter.

I know that sounds like an amazing God sent light bulb moment, and trust me it was! What did I choose to do with it might you ask? Did I start to work researching every scripture I could, digging into the word and taking notes to begin the chapter? Say thank you God! That is an amazing idea and thinking about the daunting task ahead of me and put it off for a month? Do you think you have an answer? Did I give it away with my witty choices? Yes, you are right, I decided to high five God (like he needed my high five) and go on about my busy life using excuse after excuse choosing not to put the work in to write the words the Lord has given me.

Therefore, that leads me to the part when I reassure you God is patient. He waited for me to come to Him. Don't get me wrong there were plenty of subtle hints along the way. Maybe a reference or two during a sermon at church about following the path God has planned for you. A Christian song about not giving excuses and pushing through, and don't get me wrong it was always on my mind but I still hid from the task God had laid out before me and had basically gift wrapped in a pretty pink bow. Until tonight, I sat in my bed tonight riddled with loneliness, and sadness that tends to creep in from time to time. The enemy was really working on me hard. Every channel I flipped to either had a sappy love story on or a steamy sex scene. Both of which I so desired but have no sights of either. I guess it just comes with the territory of being a Christian single mom. So, as I lay here in bed missing what I used to have, hoping for what I'm not sure I want, I fight the enemy, I fight the thoughts and feelings that try to trump the promise I know God made to me. "For I know the plans I have for you declares the Lord, plans prosper you and not to harm you, plans to give you hope and a future". I know He says I am going to have an amazing future but boy is it lonely and heartbreaking in the meantime.

As I continue my inner struggle, unable to sleep and not wanting to flip back to the food channel which will cause me to immediately go to the kitchen and eat my feelings I land upon a late night or in this case an early morning sermon. Even though I really wanted to know how that lifetime movie ended with sex and drama, I gave the enemy a quick kick in the pants and left the sermon on. And wouldn't you know it; he was preaching about putting on God's full suit of armor to help us survive this world and continue our walk with the Lord. Oddly enough he was talking about slaying the enemy with the words of truth from our God found in the Holy Bible to survive the tests and trials of our lives. Does anyone reading that think that is was a coincidence? If you do then you definitely were not in my room as I sat and listened to this sermon, immediately prayed and words flowed through my head for this chapter.

I often think of how God speaks to us. I have heard of so many analogies about the Lord speaking and us, being obedient. I, as a former third grade teacher always think of stories, and when God speaks to me I think of the 3 little pigs. When He is working in your life, guiding and directing you or asking something of you He will politely knock on the door. And if you don't answer the door and pretend you aren't home, there might be a huffing and puffing (just enough to grab your attention). Usually at this time most of us are saying, "ok God, I get it, I'll do it!" but for those of us that on occasion continually ignore the Lord at our doorstep, sometimes it takes the Lord to blow your house down before you sit up and take notice. Luckily, as I pray more often I am trying to be more obedient. This was certainly a case of huffing and puffing, but I got the message loud and clear and I thank God that I did.

So as I write this at now, 2:02 am, I can thank God that He has inspired me and written the word that can help us to survive this life and not only survive it but to use it to give us hope, strength, love, compassion and a future that the Lord already had planned for us. Let's suit up in our armor from God and not only give the enemy a black eye but slay him with turning to God and his promises of hope in our time of need and struggle.

Suit of Armor:

Finally, be strong in the Lord and in his mighty power. Put on the full armor of God, so that you can take your stand against the devil's schemes. For our struggle is not against flesh and blood, but against the rulers, against the authorities, again the powers of this dark world and against the spiritual forces of evil in the heavenly realms. Therefore put on the full armor of God, so that when the day of evil comes, you may be able to stand your ground, and after you have done everything, to stand. Stand firm then, with the belt of truth buckled around your waist, with the breastplate of righteousness in place, and with your feet fitted with the readiness that comes from the gospel of peace. In addition to all this take up the shield of faith, with which you can extinguish all the flaming arrows of the evil one. Take the helmet of salvation and the sword of the spirit, which is the word of God. And pray in the spirit on all occasions withal kinds of prayers and requests. With this in mind, be alert and always keep on praying for all the Lord's people. 2 Corinthians 4: 16-18

When you need: Hope My absolute favorite (that has picked me up off the floor, the bottom of the shower, and helped me walk to my seat from the alter)

"For I know the plans I have for you, declare the Lord, plans to prosper you and not to harm you. Plans to give you hope and a future." Jeremiah 29:11

"So we do not lose heart. Though our outer self is wasting away, our inner self is being renewed day by day. For this light momentary affliction is preparing for us an eternal weight of glory beyond all comparison, as we look not to the things that are seen but to the things that are unseen. For the things that are seen are transient, but the things that are unseen are eternal." 2 Corinthians 4: 16-18

Blessed be the God and Father of our Lord Jesus Christ! According to his great mercy, he has caused us to be born again to a living hope through the resurrection of Jesus Christ from the dead. 1 Peter 1:3

Through him we have also obtained access by faith into this grace in which we stand, and we rejoice in hope of the glory of God. More than that, we rejoice in our sufferings, knowing that suffering produces endurance, and endurance produces character, and character produces hope, and hope does not put us to shame, because God's love has been poured into our hearts through the Holy Spirit who has been given to us. Romans 5:2-5

For in this hope we were saved. Now hope that is seen is not hope. For who hopes for what he sees? But if we hope for what we do not see, we wait for it with patience. Romans 8:24-25

But those who hope in the Lord will renew their strength. They will soar on wings like eagles; they will run and not grow weary, they will walk and not be faint. Isaiah 40:31

You will be secure, because there is hope; you will look about you and take your rest in safety. You will lie down, with no one to make you afraid, and many will court your favor. But the eyes of the wicked will fail, and escape will elude them; their hope will become a dying gasp. Job 11: 18-20

He save the needy from the sword in their mouth; he saves them from the clutches of the powerful. So the poor have hope, and injustice shuts its mouth. "Blessed is the one whom God corrects; so do not despise the discipline of the Almighty." Job 5: 15-18

God's voice thunders in marvelous ways; he does great things beyond our understanding. Job 37:5

In peace I will lie down and sleep, for you alone, Lord, make me dwell in safety. Psalm 4: 8

But let all who take refuge in you be glad; let them ever sing for joy. Spread your protection over them that those who love your name may rejoice in you. Surely, Lord, you bless the righteous; you surround them with your favor as with a shield. Psalm 5: 11-12

The Lord is a refuge for the oppressed, a strong hold in times of trouble. Those who know your name trust in you, for you, Lord, have never forsaken those who seek you. Psalm 9: 9-10

But God will never forget the needy; the hope of the afflicted will never perish. Psalm 9: 18

You, Lord, hear the desire of the afflicted; you encourage them, and you listen to their cry, defending the fatherless and the oppressed, so that mere earthly mortals will never again strike terror. Psalm 10:17-18

Therefore my heart is glad and my tongue rejoices; my body also will rest secure, because you will not abandon me to the realm of the dead, nor will you let your faithful one see decay. You make known to me the path of life; you will fill me with joy in your presence, with eternal pleasures at your right hand. Psalm 16: 9-11

I call on you, my God, for you will answer me; turn your ear to man and hear my prayer. Show me the wonders of you great love, you who save by your right hand those who take refuge in your from their foes. Keep me as the apple of your eye; hide me in the shadow of your wings from the wicked who are out to destroy me, from my mortal enemies who surround me. Psalms 17:6-9

In my distress I called to the Lord; I cried to my God for help. From his temple he heard my voice; my cry came before him, into his ears. Psalm 18: 17-19

He rescued me from my powerful enemy, from my foes, who were too strong for me. They confronted me in the day of my disaster; but the Lord was my support. He brought me out into a spacious place; he rescued me because he delighted in me. Psalms 18: 6

Now this I know; The Lord gives victory to his anointed. He answers him from his heavenly sanctuary with the victorious power of his right hand. Some trust in chariots and some in horses, but we trust in the name of the Lord our God. Psalm 20: 6-7

I remain confident of this; I will see the goodness of the Lord in the land of the living. Wait for the Lord; be strong and take heart and wait for the Lord. Psalm 27: 13-14

We wait in hope for the Lord; he is our help and our shield. In him our hearts rejoice, for we trust in his holy name. May your unfailing love be with us, Lord, even as we put our hope in you. Psalm 33: 20-22

The Lord is close to the broken hearted and saves those who are crushed in spirit. The righteous person may have many troubles, but the Lord delivers him from them all; he protects all his bones, not one of them will be broken. Evil will slay the wicked; the foes of the righteous will be condemned. The Lord will rescue his servants; no one who takes refuge in him will be condemned. Psalms 34: 18-19

Samantha Gustafson

Chapter 5

Eyes Wide Open

Ever wish you could be one of the many miracles we read about all through the Bible? Where Jesus walks up to you and heals you? Better yet, all we have to do is touch a thread from His robe and we are healed of any disease, illness, ailment, depression, or hurt? What it must've been like to live and see Jesus walk the Earth healing people and bringing glory to the name of God.

Sometimes I often think to myself if only it were that easy, I could pray away any pain, suffering, worrying or troubles but it just doesn't work like that. Certainly I have faith that God can do anything in His power, but I also am aware that He is in control and the plan is far greater than what I can see in this moment in my life. He may be saving me from future heartbreak or closing that door on a relationship to open another one even greater. It's difficult to walk through those moments with faith. We just left a chapter full of scriptures to help us walk through those moments but I have to share a perspective from a pastor I listened to recently on a sermon he preached. Pastor Steven Fertick is an amazing man of God with inspiring messages and I had the pleasure of seeing him in person. I love going to my word and soaking up every ounce of knowledge and understanding I can but sometimes, hearing someone's interpretation with the help of the Holy Spirit can be so helpful.

God's word is always right on time…isn't it? Not that I am trying to jump all around in my thought process and loose you (I promise I'll get right back to Pastor Fertick's message) but I think it is so important to think about how on time God's word really is. Ever notice that you run into someone throughout your day that has the right thing to say at the right time? Or maybe the second you switch on the radio, the station is play a song that resonates with what you have been struggling with. Perhaps, it is a sign on the side of the road or an encounter with a stranger that made you think "hey that was weird." I believe that these are all ways that God communicates with us on a daily basis.

As I have been in my walk with the Lord, sometimes it is hard to describe these moments to other people that do not have faith in God. They often look at me with the supportive yet she's is crazy look and to be quite honest sometimes I feel like I'm crazy. Times when I get excited about sharing a connection I made with a lady in the check-out line or a sign or song that happened throughout my day. Or even a scripture that I read at just the right time, or a sermon that was hitting exactly what I have been struggling with. Of course, as I share these stories with overwhelming excitement, I get a mixed variety of reactions. From wow, where is the girl we used to know that was only a little bit crazy or she is on fire for the Lord. You can probably bet which category gets more participation. Needless to say it has made me think and wonder how it is that other people don't have the same experiences I seem to have on a daily basis. Am I crazy? Am I making this up? Am I hallucinating? Or am I possibly just...blessed.

Well, because I know God, and God doesn't make crazy, and I know Jesus and Jesus would save me if I were crazy I am going to do the teacher thing and cross that off the list. To be honest, hallucinations are really not on the table either so the only explanation as to why I have all of these amazing ah ha moments or joyful encounters throughout the day is because I am blessed. Mind you I am not blessed because I am anyone special, I am blessed because God had already chosen me, and like He chose you and I have finally made the choice to choose Him back.

That takes me back to my previous statement about how others don't have this same experience on a daily basis like me and why that may be. Maybe you are one of those people that don't have many encounters of joy and eye-opening experiences of God's love walking throughout your day or maybe you are someone who has them way more than me. It doesn't really matter where are you are in your walk but that your walk has started. Maybe if you are one of those people that don't get to have those encounters where God speaks through people, places and things to you throughout your day then today is your lucky day because I have the secret to get you there. Accept Him! Accept Jesus as your personal savior and He will speak to you, He will guide you and direct you and you will hear from Him and your eyes will be opened to all the beauty, love and joy he has to offer.

Now that my eyes have been opened and the veil has been lifted I am able to look back on my life even before I personally knew God or my savior and see ways He was working in my life before I even knew Him. He was there all along! Isn't it funny how hindsight is 20/20? We can look back to the past and go "oh God, I get it, you are so smart, and if I hadn't gone through _____ then I wouldn't have been able to _____". Anybody have those moments? These are the moments you know you are saved, when you can SEE, as if you have been blind your whole life and now Jesus has provided the miraculous healing to open your eyes and let you see his plan for you up until this point. I will show you how that same person who cannot still see and is blinded by his or her own human control would take the same situation. "Why does _____ always happen to me? I don't understand... I never get to _____; I'm always dealing with _____."

Now I am sure we have all been on the second end of that, blinded, guarded, jaded, lack of understanding, mistrust and even angered by our present and past situations. If you are still there I encourage you to look to the Lord and ask Him to open your eyes to His plan for you and accept what He shows you. Once the veil is lifted you have a brand new lease on life. The situations that shaped my entire being and caused the pain that I still deal with today have been made so clear to me now.

As I write, I feel like it is important to share pieces of myself so that you may see how different life can be once the veil has been lifted and my eyes have been opened. I do this in hopes that it may help someone else or give them hope that God performs miracles every day and we often overlook them. I know that He is opening my eyes and lifting the veil of oppression and lack of understanding was a miracle I will forever be grateful for.

I won't share all of my testimony here; as it will be shared later but my father passed away when I was six years old. He was 28 and I was left to be raised by my very young and very broken single mom. I love my mom dearly, and later in the book you will meet her, but life had dealt her many cards and every person deals with those cards differently. In a much-shortened version, life was not always easy. Being a single parent is hard enough but being a child raised by a single parent is difficult too. As a child, I saw things and was exposed to many things that haunt me still to this day. However, there is a silver lining to the cloud that hung ever so low throughout my life. After my husband died and I gave my life to the Lord he asked me to do one thing. That was to write my life story. So I did, I sat at the computer one night and for 3 nights in a row I didn't sleep, I wrote. Every detail, I had hidden for years from the world, every hurt and every ounce of pain. I wrote about things I thought I had forgotten, things I thought I had buried so deep they would never be thought of again. Then I wrote about feelings I didn't even know that I had. I don't believe you have to be a great writer to get things out, to express your feelings or to open up but that is exactly what God had called me to do. He called me to open myself and expose myself to be venerable and I listened.

Once I had done that it was almost a metaphorical change, almost instantaneous that my eyes were open. By opening up my past and being willing to let that go and give my past to God, He showed me why I went through what I did, and why He allowed a child to endure such moments in life. When I was in high school and old enough to understand what God was and how He worked, I often questioned if there was a God why would he put a kid though the things I had been through. Didn't He protect the children from hurt and pain? Didn't He care? Without Him even saying a word, all He had to do was lift the veil I had over my eyes for me to see that each of those trials He let me walk through made me and shaped me to be the person I am today. The young woman, the single mom, the widow, the teacher, the friend, the helper and the servant of God

Oh how thankful I was for that moment. All of the anger and frustration I had carried my whole life of why me and don't you care, or my favorite, why aren't you helping me? Was thrown out the window and replaced by thank you. Thank you for slowing building me to be the woman I need to be in this moment because you knew that my husband would die young, you knew that I would need to know how to be a single mom and what my actions would do to affect my kids. That's why you let my dad be taken from me so young, so I could relate to how my children were feeling right and how and help them in a way I never was, by turning to you.

To have the veil lifted and your eyes open to all the little moments in your day, how God may be speaking to you in a song, or through another person maybe or perhaps, in a dream, is one of the most awesome gifts the Holy Spirit can give you. But you can only recognize those gifts if you have accepted that you are no longer in control, that God is in control and the Jesus is your savior.

I challenge all those reading this to examine your lives and really think about all the goodness and mercy God has shown you in your life. Sometimes being still and reflective is a great place to be especially if you happen to be in a place of struggle. Looking at where you have come from and praying for God to open your eyes can help you to see the world in a brand new life, full of the wonder and joy God can bring into any situation, even in the ones that seem impossible.

I know you have waiting and reading an entire chapter for me to get to the sermon from Pastor Steven Fertick inspired me to write about. So speaking again about God's word right on time, Pastor Fertick preached an amazing message about "seeing it through." He used the story of Elisha and his servant.

And the king of Israel sent to the place, which the man of God told him and warned him of, and saved himself there, not once nor twice. [11]Therefore the heart of the king of Syria was sore troubled for this thing; and he called his servants, and said unto them, Will ye not shew me which of us is for the king of Israel? [12]And one of his servants said, None, my lord, O king: but Elisha, the prophet that is in Israel, telleth the king of Israel the words that thou speakest in thy bedchamber. [1] And he said, Go and spy where he is, that I may send and fetch him. And it was told him, saying, Behold, he is in Dothan. [14]Therefore sent he thither horses, and chariots, and a great host: and they came by night, and compassed the city about. [15]And when the servant of the man of God was risen early, and gone forth, behold, an host compassed the city both with horses and chariots. And his servant said unto him, Alas, my master! How shall we do? [16]And he answered, Fear not: for they that be with us are more than they that be with them. [17] And Elisha prayed, and said, LORD, I pray thee, open his eyes, that he may see. And the LORD opened the eyes of the young man; and he saw: and, behold, the mountain was full of horses and chariots of fire round about Elisha. [18] And when they came down to him, Elisha prayed unto the LORD, and said, Smite this people, I pray thee, with blindness. And he smote them with blindness according to the word of Elisha. 2 Kings 6: 10-18

In his message he quoted these scriptures to give us a picture of faith in action, the difference in faith between the God fearing prophet Elisha and his humble servant. All of the comments that I make about this sermon are based on the inspiring words Pastor Fertick preached that hit me so strongly and powerfully and continue to do so today. He mentioned that as the servant looked on to this sea of trouble, this impending army that was there to destroy him he approached Elisha with fear and defeat, not knowing where to turn or what to do. However, Elisha, who we know could've prayed for anything, prayed, *"LORD, I pray thee, open his eyes, that he may see."* (2 Kings 6:17) Naturally so, the Lord opened his eyes to see what Elisha knew to be there all along, the reinforcement of God's love and glory to save His people from the destruction that could've been.

What resonated with me when I listened to the sermon was not the triumphant story of how God always has our backs. How many times to we read and hear those encouraging words from others and dismiss them just as quickly as we received them. "Where was He today?" "I'm not worthy of that kind of protection." I speak this because I often feel that way, even though I know the power, glory and love of our God, I still find it difficult to see the light at the end of the tunnel or even envision an end at all. So as I sat and watched this sermon unfold before me it was that moment of light bulbs going off, of bells ringing or the euphoric ah ha moment every teacher lives for. We have to see it through!

He did a visual demonstration of exactly what was happening in that moment. God placed his army on the outside of Elisha and the army against him, the trouble that threatened his life but God didn't place His army in between them. It took Elisha's faith and prayer for his servant to see the help was on the other side. If he could look through the army of men sent to cause their demise he could see that God's army was more powerful, more equipped and even greater in multitude than they would ever need to not only survive the conflict but come out victorious.

If you are anything like me in moments like this when God makes it so clear through a person, sermon, message, song or interaction we tend to still try to dismiss it. Often thinking man, I wish I could've seen that army, and then I would have the faith. But in that second when the word of God reached the depths of my soul I realized that scripture was in place to lead us to just ask for our eyes to be opened. God doesn't promise to protect us from every ounce of trouble or enemy against us but He does equip us for battle and it takes our faith to see it though.

That was the heart of Pastor Fertick's message, God doesn't step in between us and the trouble that we face, which could be anything; financial issues, family, stress, anger, fears, illness, the list could go on and on but He does reassure us that what He gives us from the Holy Spirit inside us and the army and support He has if we have the faith to see it through can carry us not only through those trials but arriving victorious on the other side. That my friends are for His glory. What greater of a modern day miracle can you have than a person that others see going through an immense trial or tribulation and you bear witness to God seeing them through because they used their faith to see it through? Isn't that our purpose? Isn't that why God created us in His image? To bring Him glory and honor. What a proud father He must be when we look to Him in those weakest of moments and ask for our eyes to be opened to see the plan He laid out before us.

Before you write me off and think this is just some feel good author writing about how great she is to use the word to overcome adversity and can conquer all doubt, fear, anxiety and darkness with a glare and roll on with her day, think again. I am not that person; I have personally suffered the attack from the enemy and not just in circumstance but physically and let me tell you it is an eye opening experience. But that is an experience I give God all the glory for. He allowed that to happen to me to keep me focused on His will and His work and more importantly to show His strength and power over anything else that may come against us.

You, dear children, are from God and have overcome them, because the one who is in you is greater than the one who is in the world. 1 John 4:4 (NLT)

Jesus has conquered the world and fought against everything that we could possibly be up against and yet we still doubt His power when we are fighting our own battle. We feel as though God is only present in the watching of these occurrences happening in our lives when we should realize that He is with us as they are occurring. The Holy Spirit, which was gifted to us in the absence of Jesus, is with us at all times walking with us through the trouble, trials and tribulations. You are not alone, I am not alone but the enemy wants you to feel alone. As we pray, we pray for our eyes to be open and our ears to be receptive to the word of our God so that the Holy Spirit can conquer those moments and give us the vision to see it through. So I speak from the heart and from a mother, friend, woman, teacher, leader, and follower of Christ you are not alone in your struggle. Look to these words as encouragement that there is someone else out there that is probably right next to you that feels the same, is struggling the same or under a similar attack and you will see someone that needs to have their eyes opened by the Lord. Elisha was an amazing man of God, who saw what others could not, but saw it with his faith and knew character of God. Our God who was and is and is to come, who is the same now as He was in creation.

Trust in the Lord with all you heart and lean not on your own understanding; in all your ways submit to him, and he will make your paths straight. Proverbs 3: 5-6

And I pray.

Dear Lord, please guide and protect me every day from those that may come against me. God I pray that I lean not to my own understanding but I submit myself to you with faith, knowing that you have a plan and purpose for my life. I was created for you and by you for a purpose. I am strong because you live inside of me and I pray that when I need to see the love and protection you have for me through my trials and tribulations you will reveal them to me. And I trust that when I don't need to see the why of my situation you will keep it hidden and I will continue to walk in faith. Walk with me every day Lord and thank you for all the blessings, trials and troubles Lord that I may have because I know they are for the betterment of me as well as the betterment of your kingdom. In Jesus great name I pray. Amen

Chapter 6

Hope

Being led by the Holy Spirit I am commended to write this even on the message of hope. I myself, fall very short in this area on a daily basis. Sometimes the though comes to my mind what is there left to hope in? Honestly, I feel so guilty having those thoughts when I am saved and can see as I have mentioned before the veil lifted and all God's glorious blessings. So why then can I feel hopeless when I know hope is my lifeline given to me by the creator that loves me absolutely? My answer because I still have room to grow. No one ever said the journey to the Lord was an overnight success story. No one ever said that the day you said I accept you Jesus; you were magically transformed into a fearless, sinless, super hero. So then why do we put ourselves on this pedestal of absoluteness, which we are certain to fall from?

Can God perform miracles and have overnight success stories? That isn't the question, of course He can but does He? Maybe on occasion and I am no one to explain, understand or judge God's work. But I can attest to my own personal life and the way God has worked in my life, He gives me the tests so I can be His testimony. Every struggle, every strife, every moment of desperation or loss, God has been right there to receive the glory from it and to grow me and build me into the woman he needs me to be and that growth isn't over.

As I lay here and write and think about the word hope and the roller coaster ride my life has been day in and day out I am reminded of just how fickle our human emotions are. I mean honestly I can look at the last week of my life (and mind you I feel as though I have it together most of the time) and I am in awe of the range of emotions and situations I have found myself in. I am not talking about epic, soap opera digest worthy situations but just life in general. From happy, over joyed and just plain elated to frustrated, overwhelmed and insecure in a matter of hours and then back again. Before you think I am crazy or have a mental illness, I urge you to examine you past week and really reflect on your own emotional roller coaster of emotions and situations in your life. Honestly most of the emotions are completely warranted but it just amazes me to think about how moveable our emotions are as humans and how constant God is with his.

God's love, forgiveness, mercy and grace are immovable. The King James Version has these scriptures to reveal God's character to us.

"Every good gift and every perfect gift is from above, and cometh down from the Father of lights, with

whom is no variableness, neither shadow of turning." James 1:17

"Then this message which we have heard of him, and declare unto you, that God is light, and in him is no darkness at all." 1 John 1:15

"But the comforter, (which is) the Holy Ghost, whom the Father will send in my name, he shall teach you all things, and bring all things to your remembrance, whosoever I have said unto you." John 14:26

"Fear thou not; for I am with thee; be not dismayed; for I am thy God; I will strengthen thee; yea, I will help thee; yea, I will uphold thee with the right hand of my righteousness." Isaiah 41:10

"I am the alpha and the Omega, the Beginning and the End, says the Lord, 'who is and who was and who is to come, the Almighty." Revelation 1:8

"For God so loved the world that he gave his one and only son, that whoever believes in him shall not perish but have eternal life." John 3:16

"For by him all things were created, in heaven and on earth, visible and invisible, whether thrones or dominions or rulers or authorities all things were created through him and for him." Colossians 1:16

"The Lord will fight for you, and you have only to be silent." Exodus 14:14

"Be still and know that I am God. I will be exalted among the nations, I will be exalted in the Earth!" Psalm 46:10

I could honestly go on forever with scripture after scripture detailing the amazing character of God, from His power, grace, mercy, love, peace, comfort, forgiveness and glory. All of these scriptures bring me right back to the hope that I need, the hope I depend on, I count on to survive each day. Some days, I really look hard at my life and realize I am tired of just surviving, I want to thrive! Goodness gracious, can I just get off the roller coaster, step off the platform and walk toward the concession stand for a nice cool, refreshing drink?

You ever have those days? Where you just need a break and a nice cool drink out of the beating down sun of our existence? It is in those days I have to draw nearer to God. I have to dig and claw and scrape for His word to keep me going and to refill my hope, joy, laughter and usually without a doubt my sanity. So as I mature in the Lord and really take a step back and examine my life I realize I am definitely not in control but I know the one who is and He loves me, so I guess, let's do this!

So many times while we are going through those moments, mature Christians, you know the ones that have walked through these situations and have already learned to fully rely on the character of God, will tell you to have hope, turn to your faith and some of us go, "uh huh, yea, I know but…" There is always a but, this situation is too much, but I don't have time to just wait; but, I need an answer now. I look back on all those times I have said the same things, and in all honestly still find myself saying them and realize that there is no but in hope and faith. You have it, you have it deep in your core, and you know that deep down the Holy Spirit it telling you God has got this. That being said, it doesn't make walking through it a piece of cake but it does give you just the right amount of reassurance that you need to keep seeing it through.

I write this from personal experience, and not as someone who has it altogether, perhaps you may be similar to me, or maybe you will think I am a complete nutcase. However, I am walking through my life with Christ as best as I can and I have found that without the word, the hope and faith that it instills in me in those moments, I would be dead in the water. With the best of intentions, those rollercoasters of human emotions can put me in a pickle so quick it'll make your head spin. Just when I feel like I am about to drown and my emotions are swallowing me up, I realize, I am not alone. I have the Holy Spirit within me, Jesus Christ as my biggest supporter cheering me on from the sidelines and the All Mighty Father that loves me unconditionally. The most important word there is unconditionally. So why, please tell me why am I trying to deal with my emotions on my own or figure out how to handle a situation without consulting the one source I have that is all knowing, loving, forgiving, and full of grace and mercy? Sounds like a silly decision to me. Instead when walking through drama, crisis, or just plain life, do we call on the first available person in our phone list that we know we can complain to and get the answer we want. That could be a spouse, sibling, best friend, family member or even a coworker, but we all have them, that person that will listen and tell you exactly what you want to hear to make you feel all better.

How often in our lifetimes have those pieces of advice really worked out for us? Sure, don't get me wrong our loved ones would never mislead us and I have several go to people in my life that would sacrifice their own life for mine as I would for them but the point is they do not have all the qualities of our Almighty God. God knew our purpose and future before we were born, He has seen our future before we could even finish our yesterday and all of the moments that we see as causing us anxiety, stress, struggle and strife could actually be moments He is using to meld us into the people He needs us to be and to do His Kingdom work. So again, our loved ones, family, friends or coworkers that are the greatest listeners are always going to want to elevate the pain because we don't ever want to see someone suffer, but maybe the pain is exactly where God needs us to be in. Maybe the pain is helping us grow; maybe the pain is bringing us to a place of understanding or of greater comfort for a future need. God knows all this, and we have to trust in his character to breathe and walk through all the moments of our lives.

Does that make it easy? Absolutely not, it is a daily, sometimes hourly or minutely conscious decision to give God the control He needs in our lives. Sometimes we are our own worst enemies, we think we know what we need and what we need to do and God has a much greater plan already laid out. I personally have found several steps that have helped me to keep walking through every moment in life. And as I said before, I am still growing, still maturing and really every situation is so different but when I feel that fear, or anxiety, insecurity, frustration or down right deep sadness building inside me I have learned to follow these steps.

1. Prayer is the fastest way to communicate with God and He wants to hear from us, He wants us to say that He is in control and that we are obedient to His will. God deserves that Glory and He is waiting patiently on the sidelines for us to turn to Him with a smile or through tears and say God I really need you.

2. Go back to the word of God. It is funny that when I am in those moments, of course they are the most stressful times when we are too tired, or don't feel like it. But those are

the moments we need to suit up with the armor. Give God and the Holy Spirit something to work with. If you are asking for help with a situation and are obedient in prayer, give God the scripture to speak to you or read and refill on the hope, love, joy and peace that comes from our All Mighty Father.

3. Surround yourself with other followers of Christ. It was once told to me by a very dear friend you are only as successful as the people around you allow you to be. We are all human beings and there is not one perfect person in this world. So we are all going to be on those rollercoasters of human life at some point or another. But surrounding yourself with the right people are going to help to encourage you to reach back to God, to keep praying and renew your faith by going back to the Word. God is our life line and so many times in the middle of those moments that steal our joy or our peace the first thing we do is turn away from God. Having those supports and connections to hold us accountable for our thoughts and our actions in struggle is so important.

How does my everyday struggle and steps for overcoming it have to do with Hope? Well, I survive on the hope that God promises me, I rest in those weary moments on the hope that He already has it worked out. Knowing the character of our

God and relying on it helps to build that hope and provide the light that can brighten even the darkest tunnel.

Again I rest on God's Word:

"For I know the plans I have for you' declares the Lord, plans to prosper you and not to harm you, plans to give you HOPE and a future." Jeremiah 29:11

God promises us hope for a future that is bright and that will bring Him glory and honor. All the struggle, strife, rollercoasters, loss, death, fear, anxiety, and emotions that we encounter in the meantime are all part of the plan. Yes, some we bring on ourselves with our own choices and sins but some are a part of Gods plan for us, not to punish us, as some people would have it seen but to love us. To help us to grow and mature into following our plan and purpose by faith so the blessings He has for us can be bestowed on us.

Therefore, understanding and trusting in the character of God and relying on His power can give us the hope for a brighter tomorrow, and not in the sense of everything is going to be perfect but in the sense that everything is working for the good of those that love Him. Even the adversity and struggle is for our good so have hope and faith that God is always on our side and will always prevail.

And I pray.

"Dear heavenly father, please help me to walk through my struggles with grace and understanding that you are in control. Please help to remind me through your word, that everything that you do is for my good and that your plan for me is to prosper me and give me hope and a future. God I rest in your glorious love and un-bounding mercy as I walk this journey moving closer to you and ask you to forgive me as I fall short but lift me up to know your love and character. God please instill in me the peace you give beyond understanding to have eternal hope in the All Mighty God you are and the endless faith to see this life through and give you all the glory for what you do in my life. I ask all this in Jesus great name. Amen"

Chapter 7

Testimony

"Not only so, but we also glory in our sufferings, because we know that suffering produces perseverance; perseverance, character; and character, hope. And hope does not put us to shame, because God's love has been poured out into our hearts through the Holy Spirit, who has been given to us."
Romans 5:3-5

"I consider that our present sufferings are not worth comparing with the glory that will be revealed in us."
Romans 8:18

How often in our lives do we suffer? How often do we watch those around us suffer? All we need to do is turn on the T.V and turn to the news to see devastation from one story to the next; children suffering, loss of life, war, famine, disease, epidemics, the list can go on and on. In biblical time, there was Jesus, the healer, the one they traveled miles and miles to bring an end to their suffering. One touch of His robe, one word from His mouth and they were healed and yet today we don't realize that we have that same Jesus, that same redeemer and healer but we have the Holy Spirit right inside us to guide and direct us to live full and fruitful lives.

This chapter is dedicated to God's work in our individual lives and some pretty heroic people in my life that have been brave enough to share their tests which turned to a great testimony.

"Being confident of this, that he who began a good work in you will carry it on to completion until the day of Christ Jesus." Philippians 1:6

Our tale is never over, even when some days it really feels like it could be. God is not a God of incompletion. He will continue to prune and garden us until we are completed in His work or the day Jesus comes back to us and on that promise we can rest. Before I share the testimonies of these brave people I would like to start with a prayer.

"Lord I pray that anyone reading this or having this read to them, that their heart be open and receptive to hear not only your word and truth but also are receptive to see the miracles you have performed in these people's lives. God I pray that those hearing or reading these testimonies feel and understand the reality and pain behind the stories that you have turned in to triumph and glory. God I also pray that you help them to see that they are part of your triumphant glory

and that you are working goodness in their lives to help
return victorious. I end in prayer also asking for those that
may feel as I do, inadequate, that they find comfort and peace
in you that they are loved enough to have the same change
and power in their lives because you love them enough for
that. I ask all this in Jesus's name. Amen."

Well, I suppose it's that time. The time where you felt like
you already know me and yet I am going to continue to share
who I am and what God has done in my life. So the first
testimony you will read is my own. I write from the heart and
I have to share that I wrote my testimony a little over a year
ago because God told me to forgive so I could make room in
my life for Him. It wasn't until I spend 3 sleepless nights
dredging every moment that shaped me, my emotions, my
character and my flaws that I realized what God was asking
me to do. He was asking me to write my testimony up until
that point so I can let go of the past and open myself to a
future to which he was the center, He was the compass
directing me which way to go; not my past, my experiences or
my pain. I will forever be grateful for the first encounter with
the Holy Spirit before I even knew him to be that. I am
thankful that he helped me to reach that first step closer to
God and purge what I had let control me for way to long. So
the testimony you will be reading today is an untouched
version I wrote out of obedience 3 months after I lost my
husband and when I first called on having an actual

relationship with the lord. I hope that this testimony can help someone else.

Taking God's Path:
What does that mean for me?

(A Testimony by me, Samantha Gustafson)

About Me

Let me first begin by saying I am not an author, or a professional writer. I am a person, a person much like you trying to find my path in life and doing it one day at a time. I am on a journey to discover my value, my plan, and my purpose and use my life to the fullest and I'd like to take you on that journey as well. Just like many of you, my story hasn't been an easy one to live let alone tell, but I do not want this to be a tale of woe is me. I want it to be a journey together to inspire and uplift and find hope in the little blessings in life that we all have thanks to the Lord. So that being said, please bear with my lack of writing talent and rather enjoy and share with me my story.

My name is Samantha and I am a 27-year-old widow, too bubbly for my own good, blonde (most of the time), energetic, outgoing and well, way too enthusiastic for most people to handle at any given moment in life. The funny thing is many people in life that meet me automatically assume I was a cheerleader and I have to promptly correct them that I didn't make the cheerleading squad because I didn't smile enough, as it said on my record sheet from tryouts. Aside from that, I am a very firm believer in the saying that "those that smile the most are the ones who are the saddest inside." Yup, I was one of those people. My entire life was devoted, almost to an obsession to hide the pain, fear, and grief inside. Now others, take that same pain, fear and grief and manifest it in different ways, me, I became the bubbly person you wanted to punch in the face at 8 am. That being said, my journey has been difficult, but as I mentioned before my life has been blessed beyond belief and there are SO many others that have had it far more difficult. But even in those instances, I was told once by a pastor that every story has value and if sharing my story can help just one person than that will be God's will to help that one person. I will tell you that my story has yet to end, right now as I write it is only just the beginning, but isn't that the beauty of a journey? It really is about the route you take to get to the destination. I will take you from beginning to now and I hope as we travel together on the way, my story will be worth telling; and not because I am anyone special, but because I have a desire to change the world and I believe that sharing our lives can do that. I am but a humble young woman, from a small town, with two young children trying to survive gift we call life.

The Beginning

Of course as a child, our memories of childhood are skewed. We remember the spankings we may have received or the gifts we didn't get for Christmas, or the party we couldn't go to, because those were the things that were important to us as children. As adults we often start to look back at the steps we took through our childhood. Before I begin that journey I want to share that my intention is not to dwell in the past or hurt anyone along the way but rather discover my future and take the journey to finding where that may lead me. My mother was very young when she conceived me. She was a teenage girl from a difficult home who ran away to find love. She found that love with a slightly older, attractive bad boy type. My mom is a great person and has a heart of gold so when I speak of her it is with love and now as an adult with utter understanding but as a child I held nothing but discontentment and anger for her choices and lifestyle. Not long after the tumultuous couple began dating I was conceived. A quickie wedding was held at 8 months after conception and a beautiful, healthy baby girl was born in July exactly 4 days shy of my mother's 19th birthday.

Many children don't have memories of their parents or life from those young ages but I have a few. My parents were obviously young and both had many issues personally and together they were not helpful to one another. My father was doting and loving to me, but he also enjoyed having fun and living the single life, which obviously didn't work with my mom. The demons and addiction that plagued my dad, along with the deep seeded emotional issues my mom was facing led to some of the only memories I have of my parents.

I was probably 3 or 4 sitting atop a dryer looking into the bathroom hiding as I watched my dad pin my mom up against the wall by the throat. I didn't know if that night was going to be the night he killed her. I try to think about good memories I may have but I always seem to have trouble distinguishing pictures that could've turned into happy memories and real memories, but you always know the bad ones that keep you up at night are real because no one took pictures of those. As individuals my parents were great people. As far as I have been told my dad was a very hard worker, good looking and life of the party. My mom has a heart of gold, misguided sometimes but will work her fingers to the bone if required.

Needless to say my parent's relationship didn't work out. My mom spent the rest of her time trying to find Mr. Right that would complete our family and love her. Again, I love my mother to death and we all have flaws, my mom's looking for love in all the wrong places. There were several options after my dad, all of which the same M.O. abusive, alcoholic and crazy. Though seeing all of this and being a part of it, I spent every other weekend with my dad and most of my time with my mom. She worked so hard to be the best mom she was capable of being at the time. And then it happened. Time and probably lifestyle caught up with our family. I was 6 years old, and it was my dad's weekend to have me. I waited on the porch of the guy's house my mom was dating at the time waiting for daddy to pick me up. Mom called me into the house and said that daddy wasn't coming but he promises to pick me up on Sunday to take me roller-skating. Well as a kid that is all it took, roller-skating it is!

Little did I know he wanted his Saturday night free. I am not going to speculate the reason and I am sure that many people reading this know more than I do and will probably get upset at my speculation but as a child, does it really matter the reason? He wasn't with me. In the time my mom and dad were separated, dad had moved on and there was a half-brother for me right down the road from my current living place. Well, Sunday morning I woke up bright and early, bounced out into the living room and beamed from ear to ear and said to my mom "its Sunday! My daddy is taking me skating!" I know that I said these exact words because my mom has replayed that moment every day since in her mind for the past 20 years. As I looked at her crying I had no idea what was wrong. She didn't say a word and asked me to get dressed and told me we were going to my grandparents' house (my dad's parents). So I did as I was told and even as a six year old I can remember every moment like it is etched in my brain after that. I walked into my grandparents' kitchen and everyone was crying hysterically and looking at me trying to hold it back and crying again.

My mom walked over to my Uncle Scott and asked him if he would tell me. We went for a walk and he told me that my dad was in heaven and he was an angel now. Of course as a 6-year-old kid I had no concept of heaven or even that dad wasn't there. My dad had gone to a party the night before and died drinking and driving, he was supposed to have me. To be perfectly honest, other than the occasional "missing daddy" moments his death really didn't hit me until much later in life. As a child I had no idea the repercussions that would have for my life, feelings and family.

Even attending his funeral didn't help me to understand he wasn't coming back. I can remember exactly the position he was in, the cards and pictures that my cousins laid atop him, the funeral home, the smells, the people and the pain but I didn't feel or understand any of it. I even got in trouble for running around joyfully. Kids lose their parents every day, and some for more noble reasons than others but losing my dad was the beginning step in my life that would forever shape the person that I am today and it was only just the beginning. The first few years after losing my dad, I don't know if medication was helpful or therapy and I really have never gotten into that deep of a conversation with my mom, although I have my suspicions, but she was amazing from what I can remember.

Times weren't always easy; she was a young, widowed mother with limited education and on her own. Sure, she still wanted to go out and be young and have fun, but there was food on the table, a roof over our heads and she worked at any job she could find. She would pick up eggs in hen houses, wax and wash boats, clean houses; if it were manual labor she could do it. I will never forget in the 4th grade I wrote a paper about my mom. It didn't matter to me that she carried me along to bars and karaoke pool halls because I respected her for taking care of me. In my paper, the teacher had asked what we respect most about our moms and I wrote "that she isn't scared of any man she can hit them right back." Now looking back, if I would've received that from one of my students, probably would've thrown up a red flag, but for me at the time I really did respect my mom for holding her own and taking care of me because she was all I had left. Then the trouble began again, that looking for love in all the wrong places.

After my dad passed away my amazing paternal grandparents started taking me every other weekend in their place. Therefore, these were kid free weekends against my mom's will. What does one do that is lonely with a looking for love complex? Find it, in all the worst places possible. Although spending that time with my family was literally one of the best experiences of my life because it shaped me into wanting that traditional family more than anything in this world, it was probably the cause of the demise of my mom and mine's relationship. She was lonely, hurt, confused and depressed. She had lost my dad suddenly, was a single parent, young and overwhelmed and most importantly lonely. So we began the pattern that will never end and I am sad to say hasn't ended yet. One abusive (physically, mentally and emotionally) jerk after another. Sometimes parents can be blind to what their actions do to their children. I believe this is one of those cases. My mom and I have grown to have understanding in recent years but she still doesn't understand that I was in those rooms hiding under beds, in closets and sneaking back in houses to collect our stuff while she was being pummeled to the point of no return. I was there watching her drink out of straws with her jaw wired shut. I was there to deal with the emotional fallout when she reached her lowest of low. I was there when she had two more children with someone she knew wasn't right for her. I was there through it all, on couches in strange houses, in cold cars, in desperate lifesaving moments.

I grew to be her protector. To pull couches in front of doors and sleep there so I would be the first to know if the person came back because she was scared to call the police. My mom didn't trust the world, and I guess rightfully so because the world had let her down to many times. Because she didn't trust the world, I had no one to turn to for help when I couldn't help her let alone help myself. I grew up in this world of hurt, pain, mistrust, and most importantly fear. And not just fear of men but fear of being alone, being hurt, begin unloved. I never saw love, real love and if people did love me I shut them out before they could ever decide not to love me again. But through it all my friends, people at school, people in the community saw a bright eyed, friendly, energetic little blonde girl with good grades and a great life. Oh how looks can be deceiving.

All Grown Up

As the years went on I became programmed to lie about my feelings to hide my pain and not to trust anyone not to hurt you. Everyone is out to hurt you, and if you let them in that is exactly what will happen. It is almost laughable to think about middle school into high school. No one knew where I came from or even a fraction of what I had seen or been through. It is almost funny to think back to pivotal moments in life but I will never forget one of my friends in middle school. I had finally opened up to her about a tiny little piece of my life and she looked at me and said "Sam, I had no idea that you didn't have a dad, I thought you were a preppy kid with money and a good life." I literally laughed out loud and thought to myself, this is a little scary how good I am at this.

I am sure that many of you reading this coming from abusive homes where the normal becomes learning to be good at hiding. Sure there were a few close calls with people trying to take you away but you are taught that if you talk you might go to a place far worse than where you are now so keep your mouth shut, people have it a lot worse off. And so I did. I became the person that hid the pain with a pretty smile and pretended to be completely normal. I tried to get through normal teenage girl issues, bullying, boys and clothes. Through all of this hiding I never let anyone in.

There was one person in my life, my Aimee. Aimee and I met at Bible school as young children and became lifelong best friends, well sisters when I moved in around the corner in 5th grade. But at this point in life, even Aimee didn't know the half of it. Trust me, you could tell some of it if you spend 5 seconds in our home but the past was the past and only I carried it with me. So I grew up, strong, independent, a caregiver for my mom emotionally and guarded as a person. I craved love and my only concept of love was from movies. You know what I am talking about, hopeless romantic; sweep you off your feet kind of love. Like I had mentioned I had never seen a functional relationship let alone been a part of one so that was the only concept I had and I was going to run with it as far as I could.

By the time I hit high school the talks had begun about the rest of your life. All of my friends were choosing careers and colleges and setting their sights on parties and fun. My goal, I wanted to be a wife, mother and have a family. I wanted

Sunday spaghetti dinners, Easter egg hunts, love and family. I know, strange for a 14-year-old kid but I needed it more than you will ever know. The relationship that my mom had found herself in the past several years off and on leading up to high school were very abusive and dysfunctional on both sides, and it definitely wasn't one or the other but mom always seemed to pick guys and relationships that brought the worst out in each other.

She got pregnant, so the summer leading up to my freshman year I was parent to the baby who had a daddy that ran and a mom who was not prepared to be a single parent again. Again, wearing the rose colored glasses my mom thought she had finally found her mate, the one she'd grow old with. Instead she found a runner who never wanted children in the first place and now, again I am a caretaker/father/husband/sister and teenager all at once, if you can decipher that. Needless to say by my freshman year in high school I was looking for someone to love me. Someone who wanted to take care of me and who would sweep me off my feet and that was when God literally sent me Brett.

My angel on Earth

Up until this point both my mom and history had shown me if you want to catch a guy dress cute, flaunt it and give him whatever he wants because this obviously worked for my mom. I got on the school bus my freshman year of high school dressed to impress. I had been up since about 4:30, had my hair all curled up in an up do (apparently I was going to prom instead of homeroom) makeup done to the nine and cute clothes. Then I saw him, this really cute farmer looking kid with blonde hair, blue eyes and a dark green LL.Bean book bag. We made eye contact and that was it, I was in love. I know, crazy right. Well very long story short this kid wanted nothing to do with me. Wouldn't talk to me, despite my obvious attempts every day to get his attention and turn on all of the charm I thought I had. So I did what any cute freshman girl would do, I joined the soccer team as a manager and met some really cute soccer players.

It was better than going home right afterschool and isn't social networking with the right people the most important part of high school? So I dated a few boys in the fall, well I guess dating was holding hands and passing notes in the hallway, but I could not stop thinking about this boy. His cousin was so nice to me and we all rode the same bus so I decided to ask for inside information. How do I get his attention? Ryan, his cousin told me I wasn't country enough for him. Yup, that was all it took. I country it up, I wore my hair down, less makeup and more references to riding 4 wheelers in the conversation. It took my whole freshman school year to get up the confidence to start talking to Brett.

By baseball season I was ready to get his attention. Though my home life made it very difficult to do anything at all, I was able to go to a few of his baseball games. My mom wouldn't let me go anywhere because she was back on with Mr. Right, aka baby daddy and wanted me home to help with my brother while she visited Mr. Right. However, as fate would have it, my best friend/sister Aimee had a brother on Brett's baseball team. Therefore, I could catch a ride to games. Brett and I began talking and it took one very short attention grabbing skirt and lots of flak from his teammates for him to finally asked me if I wanted the title of being his girlfriend.

My mom instantly loved Brett, probably more than she loved me because as she would say, I was so lucky to find someone like him, because she never did. I knew I was lucky, he was everything you would want in another person, responsible, hardworking, caring, kind, loving, financially savvy (aka frugal), respectful, loyal and above all he valued family values and traditions. I knew I was going to marry him whether he knew it or not. Then he took me home to meet his family. Quite possibly the best family anyone could ask for, they ate together, laughed together, sang together, worshiped together and were the quintessential hard working, close-knit farm family. What more could a girl ask for?

Throughout high school, every difficult moment really doesn't faze me now because I look back and knew that I had Brett. Things weren't easy, mom married Mr. Right, they were abusive to each other, I was an outsider in our home and not welcomed. They decided it was a great idea to bring another child into that. I think I left my "family" emotionally the day I met Brett. I couldn't walk away from that chapter because now, I was not only protecting my mom but I also had the responsibility of protecting my little brothers. Without getting into the tale of woe, it wasn't great. Needless to say, God gives you exactly what you need when you need it, and He gave me Brett.

Brett was supportive and took on the crazy with me, he loved me for who I was and what I was dealing with. Any other 17-year-old kid would have run in a heartbeat and he never left me, not one time did he try to back out or give up. I would have done anything to make him happy, to make him love me forever. He was my everything! Our relationship continued to grow stronger and how could it not, he was the first person in my life I let in completely without reservation. He knew my past and saved me from my present. I left my home the day I turned 18 because 1 minute sooner and the police would have been called like the many times before when I tried to leave that dangerous situation.

It is funny what you remember, because honestly sometimes I choose to forget. But I will never forget one day in high school sitting in algebra class. It was the anniversary of the day my dad died and this girl was just non-stop bulling me from behind. I finally couldn't take it anymore, I wrote her a note saying, thank you for making the day my dad died so much better, handed it to her and walked out of class. I went to the nearest bathroom, cried, got myself together and went to my next class. People still had no idea I wasn't some well to do preppy kid. What can I say, I am a good pretender!

Sitting in my next class I get called to the guidance office. I walk in and the bully was sitting on the couch bawling her eyes out. Utterly confused I asked what I am doing there. The counselor proceeds to tell me that the bully is really sorry and that I don't understand what she has been through in her life. I proceed to take a step back and fill her in on a small portion of my life and struggles to where the bully stops crying with her jaw on the floor and the counselor replying to me, "I can't believe you are not pregnant or on drugs or dropped out of school, you know those are the statistics."

Yup, that is one of those defining moments in life and before you judge this poor woman, in her defense I had the facade of having the perfect life in school, no one knew anything, because they didn't have to and it was safer that way so I am sure that she was just as flabbergasted as the bully. High school was fun but I was living a different life behind closed doors at home, but I always had Brett. He was my lifeline; the one I could count on and now I realize he was my miracle from God Himself.

After being poor literally my whole life and looking forward to it finally paying off my helping me get to college, I was faced with yet another obstacle, the marriage to Mr. Right which kicked me out of my home, left me emotionally damaged and alone, it also left me without options for college. So the guidance counselors my senior year became my best friends to cry with and help me apply for every scholarship known to mankind. Needless to say the competition with honor society students and athletes didn't leave room for the girl who barely had a roof and had to work afterschool to afford to take her own clothes to the laundry mat. I thought that history was going to repeat itself; I wasn't making it to college.

Then a teacher I had told me about a full ride to a nearby college to study environmental science. I was in the FFA and loved every minute but honestly I was only in it because of Brett. After I got in, it was probably one of the most rewarding opportunities I had in my life, because of this teacher I was able to get to college on a full ride for environmental science. Anyone that knows me knows that this was definitely not the career choice I belonged in. I was made to be a teacher. I spent half of my day my whole senior year volunteering at a local elementary school. But as they say you do what you have to do. I am not quite sure why I wanted to be a teacher, it obviously wasn't because I was intelligent by any means and felt I had knowledge to pass along to others, I think it was more my faith began in high school.

Chapter 7: Testimony

When you feel alone, isolated from life and the people around you, no matter what age you begin to question things. Question life, choices, other people's choices and it all brings you to the big question, what do I believe in. All through high school I had Brett, but it was new and we were young. He was an amazing addition to my life, but we were still too young for me to have everything in life figured out and determine where my life was going. As I mentioned before, my dad passed away when I was young. Grief is a very interesting feeling because there is no real definition/time limit or rules applied to one's grief. I didn't begin to really grieve my dad until I was in high school going through the life that I had always had but was finally old enough to realize wasn't right. I didn't really grieve him as a person, but more as a lack of option. "How could my life been different?" "Would he have loved me?" "Would he have wanted to change for me?" These questions plagued my every thought as the world around me crashed in and I was expected to have it all under control and tackle the world as a fourteen year old.

Again, I was a very good pretender. The years went on and the more I let Brett in and allowed him to love me and I loved him, my faith in life and humanity grew stronger. I had hopes and dreams of making a difference in the world and having a family that I could help to grow into amazing people with traditions and values. I wanted to be a part of something greater than myself. With Brett that was possible.

Samantha Gustafson

The Man That Stole My Heart and Gave Me Life

As we grew, so did our relationship and love. I'm still not quite sure why he stayed with me, I wouldn't have. I was literally the crazy girl from down the road with a whole lot of baggage and a pretty smile. There were so many girls that Brett could have chosen that would have been easier, less complicated and better for him, but he stuck with me. As we grew up and I began to open up to Brett and trust in his love I began to think about my faith again.

Relationships are never easy, and they take so much work and commitment, especially when you are young, growing and changing but Brett and I grew together. Brett was from a local farm family that were very close knit, loving and supportive of each other. He often would say the most difficult thing he ever had to go through was his parents' divorce and even that by high school was amicable. By the time I was introduced to the family his parents were great friends and co-parents. Loving and doting, Brett and his sister were healthy, happy, confident young people with the whole world at their fingertips. I envied Brett's attitude on life, and his confidence to accomplish and do anything he wanted. He never worried about how things may work out he just made them happen. I was literally in awe of him and to be honest he changed me. I really didn't know who I was as a person from the beginning.

I will refer to myself as the "great pretender." I would be and do anything anyone wanted me to be to make them happy and keep me off the radar. I hid my pain, fear and depression from the world because those are not desirable qualities and honestly I was in constant search for someone to like me or even more importantly love me. Yes, I know sad, but part of this journey is being honest with oneself and you cannot begin to heal unless you are. So as the "great pretender," Brett and I grew so strong. If he wanted to hunt or fish or crab or farm I wanted to do all of the above. If he wanted to stay home instead of going out guess what I wanted to do? Brett never asked me to change or even wanted me to, it was in me, and it was who I was. I wanted his love so badly that I would have done anything to keep it. Now looking back I see how foolish that was because all along he knew who I was and loved me unconditionally as I was. But sometimes you have to learn these lessons the hard way. Brett was a very quiet, reserved, headstrong person. If he wanted it, he got it, and if he thought it, then it was true. I valued and respected his attitude on life and his work ethic. He had a dream, a dream to build a farm and to pass on that farm and lifestyle to his children and I had a dream to be a wife and a mother and pass on the traditions of family and values. Our dreams became one, and I would have done anything, as he did to make those dreams come true.

After high school came college for me, which I eventually switched my major to elementary special education, work and life building was next for Brett. We were so young and so many people doubted every aspect of our life. Now looking back no wonder, look where I came from and what I was, no wonder people were worried about this amazing, goal-oriented person like Brett deciding at 19 to marry me. But at every turn and every hardship we preserved, I almost feel like our job in our relationship was to prove others wrong. We married at 21 and 6 months later found out we were pregnant with our first child. Yes, I know these things should not seem unexpected we all know what goes into getting pregnant but it was an unexpected gift from God.

I had just gotten hired, fresh out of student teaching a month before, we lived with his father and I had no health insurance. Brett was busy building our life for us, we were trying to build chicken houses, which at every turn seemed to blow up in our face. Then came telling everyone of our great news. Needless to say I spent much of my pregnancy alone, scared and isolated from everyone I thought to call friends. "She isn't ready." "They can't do it." "They live with their parents." "They are too young." "They don't know what they are doing."

Chapter 7: Testimony

It seems to me that right about that point in life when I start letting my guard down and letting people in, well people let you down. Many people get so frustrated with me when I refuse to let them in. Disappointment wasn't even a word you could use to describe my feelings. I had waited my whole life to find prince charming, get married and be a mom and this was not how I pictured it. I thought that people would be happy, supportive and loving but I was wrong. Through it all Brett and I grew stronger. At this time in life Brett was not big into going to church. He always had faith in the Lord but I think it was a private, quiet understanding between him and God. We would talk about the events happening in our life and Brett would always say "why do things never go right for us?" "Why does it always have to be so difficult?"

Even then, my answer would always be, "because everything happens for a reason." I will never forget the moment Brett questioned my theory. It was obviously after our glass was so full he just couldn't handle my optimism anymore and the explanation about this being part of Gods plan was not comforting. So he said to me, "Samantha, if this is God's plan and everything happens for a reason then why did your dad die?" He was not being hurtful by any means but more truthful because honestly things had gotten worse, my job was only temporary that school year, I lost my job and health insurance by June and I was 5 months pregnant, our chicken houses which needed to be built before we could start building our house were being held up and again and we were still living in the trailer his father owned with no room for a baby.

So I would say that his question was legitimate. It isn't something I hadn't thought of myself a million times before but it was something I was willing to share with him now. Going through everything I had seen and been a part of in my process of life I had come to this very thought in high school when I was at my absolute lowest of low. I questioned faith and why my life and path seemed to be so much more difficult and isolating than many others around me and then I started thinking about God. I had never been one to profess my love for the Lord or share those feelings but my faith began at that moment. I realized that I haven't had control of my life and I wasn't going to get it. There had to be something bigger than little old Samantha in this world. There had to be a plan and purpose for me. I can't possibly navigate this world on my own and I came to the conclusion that I have to trust that God is with me and everything is a part of His plan. I hadn't given my life to Him yet but I knew He was there and I at least started the foundation of coming to Him with trust.

So my response to Brett was that explanation of how I came to find God but also if my dad hadn't have passed away I wouldn't have moved to this area and I wouldn't have met him, which was literally the best thing that has ever happened to me in my life. Up until this point I always knew it could be worse and it was my job to continuously remind Brett that everything happens for a reason and it could always be worse.

Our life continued and it always found a way to get better with blessings from God. I was hired back into my position at 8 months pregnant, our chicken houses were nearing completion and our baby boy was due in the beginning of October. I could honestly support my feelings and convictions that God has a plan for our life no matter how sticky the situation gets. That doesn't mean that everything was always perfect. It always seemed that at every turn there was bound to be a struggle but isn't that life? I'm not going to bore you with all the things that happened and trials we had along the way because I am wise enough to know that all of those trials and tribulations are what make us who we are and we all have them. Even if it seems like Sally down the street has a perfect life or John Smith always seems to get the promotion. Life doesn't leave anyone out. I guess you could say I am wise beyond my years, I don't know or I just have learned about life early but whatever the case life happens to everyone.

Things are Too Perfect

At some point in our lives, probably about 10 years or so into our relationship things began to change. We had grown and survived my past; our struggles and now we seemed to have everything our dreams could ever desire. We had two beautiful, healthy children, an amazing life sustaining relationship built on communication, trust and love, a beautiful home, a functioning farm and I was in my perfect job fulfilling the work I always believed God intended of me. The next two years couldn't be more perfect. Sure, we had some slight ups and downs but in the grand scheme of life it had finally seemed to move full circle and karma seemed to be finally paying us back, but I knew better.

Life had taught me that no one can be this happy, no one gets their fairy tale so one spring day my anxiety and fear got the best of me. I reached out to my teaching partner and great friend. We had been teaching next to each other for the past two years and became instant friends. We were two peas in a pod. We begged to be placed together to team teach, her being the regular education teacher and me the special education teacher and again, the fates aligned and my life was going swimmingly so, yup, you predicted it we got our wish! That year had been magical! We were the perfect storm, helping students that had seemed to give up, making a difference in lives and enjoying every minute of the challenge together.

Our children at home were growing and healthy, our farm was thriving and Brett had even agreed and went on a family vacation to Disney in January! I had made comments to several of the people that knew some of my background in a joking manner that I am just waiting for the "other shoe to drop." Their response was always, "Sam, you have been through enough, its time things finally go right for you."

That spring day I opened up to my friend Meg. It was on our planning period and I burst out saying, "I want to start a charity," she laughed and said, "Where did that come from?" I burst into tears, I said, "Meg, everything is to perfect, it is too amazing, my life has never been this wonderful, nobody gets their happily ever after. I feel like I need to give back or help others I can't just enjoy this amazing life and not give back."

I continued to cry and tell her some things about my life and how I have had a fear since the day I fell in love with Brett that something bad is going to happen. I have carried this overwhelming fear my entire life, when is the shoe going to drop? Every pregnancy I waiting for something to be wrong with our baby, every fight I waited for Brett to leave, every evaluation at work I waited to fail and this fear multiplied by a million the more things grew stronger and more perfect. Her response was exactly what it should have been and what would be completely normal for any friend to say. She reassured me that it was ok to be happy and that nothing terrible is going to happen. If I wanted to do things for other people that was perfectly fine but not to feel like I had to just so something bad didn't happen. She then said what everyone else had already told me, that I had been through more than most people twice my age and maybe this is just my time to be happy. I went home and thought about this, maybe she was right, maybe it is finally ok to let my guard down and enjoy these moments and life that God has given me.

Then everything changed.

The Journey

During this time of complete and utter bliss we had just returned from a trip in January from Disney World, things were amazing and life was just full of blessings. Although, that lingering feeling that something could happen and will happen haunted my every waking thought. While we were in Disney I noticed a small little bump on Brett's chest right under his collarbone. I thought it was a little white head and we dismissed it. As the weeks went on and we got closer to spring break I hadn't really noticed it too much until I was giving him a kiss goodbye one morning.

We were being silly and I began to kiss his neck and pulled his collar down and noticed that it had definitely gotten bigger. Not huge by any means but bigger and you could tell that he had been bothering it, which he refused to admit. I began to nag him profusely about it saying the infamous words I'll never be able to get out of my head, "Brett, I know you don't ever go to the doctor, but this isn't just about you any more, you have me and the kids! What if its cancer?"

I have to say I am literally crying as I type this because how can one nagging wife's plea be so haunting. He finally agreed to go and by April he had an appointment with his doctor. As far as Brett admitted his Doctor didn't seem overly concerned but wanted to have it removed and biopsied just in case, "More than likely it's just a cyst," Brett said. So I relaxed and his appointment with the general surgeon wasn't for another couple of weeks.

It was the first week in June. Things were undeniably hectic at school, planning field trips and field day and it was the last week of school. I insisted on going with him to get it removed on that Tuesday in June. It was a quick procedure and I was back to school for the remainder of field day within an hour. That following Friday and possibly the most emotional day of the year for me, to say goodbye the children you love just as much as your own children and to send them off into the world to another school the next year to possibly never seem them again. Brett knew this was very difficult for me so as we kissed goodbye that morning he told me to have a great day and remember what I have done for these kids and how much of a difference I had made.

That night was like any other night. It was summer so Brett was working late in the fields and I had gotten the kids home and dinner and in bed. I was on such a high that tomorrow would begin our summer break and the kids were finally at the age that maybe just maybe we could do something. I had already bought season passes to Sesame Place and planned beach days and adventures galore and then Brett came home. He kissed me hello, went to give the boys their good night kiss and after we tucked them in he pulled me into our bedroom and as we stood in front of our closet door he stared at me. He looked so sad and upset and confused and it scared me to death I finally asked him what was wrong.

"The doctor called me yesterday afternoon," he said.

"What why didn't you tell me? What did they said?" I was panicking and confused.

"He asked me to come in this morning to talk about my results, I have cancer."

"Don't be stupid Brett that isn't funny! Why didn't you tell me? Are you joking?" I was frantic, Brett always had a knack for teasing me and making things seem worse to get me all roweled up and then bringing me down easy I just knew this was one of those things. He was joking, he wanted to see what I would say and then he'd tell me it was just a cyst and all my worrying was for nothing. But he wasn't, he looked at me and I looked at him filled with questions and we started crying.

He didn't know what kind of cancer or how bad, he was confused and said he just wanted to get out of the doctor's office and couldn't think straight to ask any questions. I of course got so upset with him. That is exactly why you take someone with you. I was your wife; I was your best friend and protector how could you not tell me. He simply looked at me through tears and said he loved me too much to make my last day of school saying goodbye to my kids harder when he was sure it was probably bad news I couldn't do anything about.

Needless to say, our lives would never be the same after that point. We spent the whole weekend talking ourselves out of it, it was Brett, he was healthy there wasn't anything wrong with him, he felt perfect, it can't be that bad. He is 28 and in perfect health for goodness sake. Monday morning I made the call. I called the nurse who had delivered the news to Brett on Friday, as soon as I introduced myself her voice flooded with concern and she immediately told me she had been thinking about us all weekend. I still couldn't understand why this person, who has never met me has such pity and sadness in her voice. So I asked the basic questions, what kind is it? What stage is it? What do we do now?

Her first answer was it is skin cancer, Melanoma. I had a sudden flood of relief. Haven't you always heard if you are going to have cancer you want skin cancer? Easily treated, people rarely die, cut if off and go. Well I was wrong and so are you if you think that. She didn't know which stage, we would have to do more testing but it was metastatic which meant that the spot they removed from his chest was not where it started.

You know, nothing brings you closer to God then when you really need a miracle. I know that isn't how it should be and you should want God in your life at all times, but doesn't it always seem to work that way? I prayed to God that night and every waking moment afterwards for this to be a dream, for us to get the miracle of having Brett's health back, our life back, our dreams back. We had a 3 year old and a 1 year old. Things like this aren't supposed to happen. In this process I have looked back and seen all of the blessings we were given. It was the end of the school year so I could go to all of his doctor's appointments and testing without fear of losing my job or choosing between my husband and our family financially. Another blessing was the kindness of every medical professional that we encountered. They say hindsight is 20/20 and now looking back I understand why everyone was so concerned and caring about expediting the testing process and getting us answers as quickly as possible. Yes, it was because they cared but they also knew how grave the situation was and we were two young, naive, in love happy parents that thought cancer was beatable.

The Struggle

One of the biggest and hardest defining moments in our journey came in the very first moments. We were still in shock, naïve and scared but not understanding. They had gotten us in for tests and blood work rather quickly and they wanted to do the full work up to find where the primary source was if it was on the skin or in his body. They were going to do a brain MRI and body PET scan to cover all the bases. It was Saturday morning at the imaging center and we were waiting for our brain MRI. The nurses assured us that even though it was a Saturday if the Doctors found something alarming they would contact us that afternoon. The imaging took about 2 hours and that weekend became the longest weekend of our lives, waiting for the phone to ring with bad news. The phone never rang.

We knew we weren't going to stay with doctors around home from the beginning since wanted to get to a university hospital that specializes in Melanoma. The doctors and nurses advised me to get a notebook and get copies of every test result, lab result and imaging disk so we will have it at the ready for any doctor at any time. We walked into the PET scan body image center with a confidence that well, let's mark off the brain because they said no news is good news and we definitely didn't get any news over the weekend. I walked to the desk, checked Brett in and they handed me a sealed envelope.

In the next moment I made the stupidest decision I had ever made in my life. I opened it. I knew the test he was getting ready to do would take about 3 hours and I thought since we already knew there was nothing in his brain, looking at the report would be no big deal and give us the reassurance we needed to get through that waiting process. As I sat down next to him in the waiting room I opened the envelope. He wasn't paying attention to me, preoccupied with a magazine he had picked up and I am fairly certain he didn't know what I had in my hand anyway. My eyes immediately went to the bold print at the center of the page that listed each tumor they found in his brain and their sizes.

There were 7 altogether. He caught my expression and the tears that immediately welled in my eyes that I quickly tried to hide and close the envelope. He asked me what was wrong but I assured him that it was nothing, but he took the paper out of my hand. It took only a split second but seemed like an eternity and then the nurse was at the waiting room door and called him back. He stood up, handed me the paper and simply told me not to cry. For the next 3 hours I waited alone hysterical walking around outside, in and out of the waiting room not only because the realization that the person I loved more than I loved myself or life itself could possibly die but because I had caused him the pain of having to lay in that machine alone thinking for 3 hours without me to hold him and us to hold each other and get through this. How could I be so stupid? How could I hurt him so bad?

That is when the blur began. The blur of diagnosis, testing, doctors, treatments options and disbelief. We had to go through the entire data collection process with our local doctors before we could be transferred and accepted by the melanoma specialists at the University of Pennsylvania. After all the testing was said and done, according to imaging locally he had 7 lesions in his brain, one in his lung, one in a lymph node under his arm and several small ones in his skin. We went to an appointment with the local radiologist who prided himself on being honest, straightforward and not sugar coating it. He looked at us in the eyes, 3 days after testing was complete, two weeks after we found out Brett had anything wrong with him and said he had 6 months to live if we were lucky and there wasn't a darn thing we could do about it.

No, no, no, no, no. Not possible, it wasn't going to happen. How could this happen? He is perfectly fine; there is nothing wrong with him! He is walking, talking, working, happy, smiling, how could he possibly be gone in 6 months? We hated this guy, I couldn't look at him, he tried to shake my hand and smile at me and all I wanted to do was rip his head off and spit down his throat. He wasn't even trying to entertain a possibility of Brett being a survivor, of Brett beating the odds. How could someone be that cold? That untrusting of the miracles that happen every day? Brett was going to be that miracle. I could get into every gruesome detail of Brett and I's journey but we all know how much dignity that can take from a person. Brett was the strongest person I have ever known and will probably ever know and he would never deserve to have that shared.

We finally got up to the University of Pennsylvania about 1 month after diagnosis. The doctors there were amazing, they were on the forefront of melanoma research and there were so many promising new drugs and options. His doctors were optimistic and I carried that optimism with me at all times. I think deep down Brett knew, I truly believe that he was giving it everything he had to stay strong for the kids and us. There was so much through this process that only Brett and I shared together. The hugs, kisses, caresses, the deep conversations and tears about what could be. The reassurance from me that will never happen, and the strength from him saying it is what it is, if it does happen. He was my rock and he made the decision not to let anyone else in on the situation and how bad it really was.

Everyone knew he had cancer but no one knew the timeline and how precarious melanoma could be. We spend the entire summer concentrating on his brain tumors, radiation and gamma knife procedure. The gamma knife was successful but when they went to do the imaging to prepare to radiate the 7 lesions the testing down home, they found 31 + additional lesions. Essentially the game had changed. We really never got good news in any way shape or form and even when we weren't expecting any news something always came up. In the midst of it all our relationship grew stronger every day.

I honestly thanked God every day for Brett letting me in, letting me help him and him letting me go through this with him. He didn't have to do that. Brett was a strong, independent individual that really could have been stubborn and turned angry and pushed me away but he didn't and we shared 6 months of pain and torture together as one. For that I will forever to be grateful. By fall it was time to head back to school, we were awaiting another round of radiation for his brain and I was trying to take my days very carefully to keep as many waiting in the wings for when things could possibly turn bad.

We had a routine visit to Penn at the end of September, when we mentioned to the doctor that Brett's left knee was getting pretty weak. She looked at us with the same concern she had when we first came to see us and ordered a spine MRI. The results were devastating; Brett's spine was inundated from top to bottom with melanoma. How could this happen? How could he have had melanoma for so long that it could literally take his entire body without a single symptom? The next hour after we found that out I went to my school district business office and began paperwork on my leave of absence.

Words cannot possibly describe the pain of watching someone you love more than you love yourself lose their life, their function and their will to live. I am not even going to describe the moments that we shared and the pain that we endured together looking into each other's eyes knowing that every moment could be our last together. Then looking at our children and having their birthday parties over the next two months trying to pretend that he will be there for the next one.

Throughout this entire journey we still tried to maintain hope, and our relationship with God. Brett came to the Lord and accepted his fate, but I hadn't, I wouldn't. I was going to find a cure and I thought for sure that if I prayed hard enough and believed in God's power enough one of these drugs would perform a miracle. You often wonder if you knew then what you knew now would you change anything and I am fairly certain that my answer would be no.

I would never have given up on thinking that he was going to be a miracle; I could have never given up on him. He never gave up on me and he loved me until his very last breath, just as I loved him. He was my rock, my savior and realized things in me that I could never see for myself. As I watched helplessly as he lost weight, lost the function in his legs and desire to live I prayed and cried harder at night and in the shower than I have ever prayed or cried in my life. I am proud to say I never once questioned God, but I tried so hard to convince Him to save the love of my life. In one quick moment everything changed.

The Friday evening in December, Brett began to have double vision, which seemed to be a side effect of the chemo drug that he had been on aggressively. He refused to go to the hospital and he reassured me that he was fine and if it got worse he'd go. There was nothing I could do or say to change his mind, he was capable of deciding what he wanted to do and just stubborn enough to follow through. I watched anxiously knowing how helpless I was and how done he was fighting the battle I wasn't sure he wanted to win anymore. We made it through Saturday with little difference and Saturday night as we lay in bed, I cried to him like I had never cried before. I told him my fear of losing him and how helpless I felt and how much I loved him. How can he make me watch him have these problems like the double vision and not let me get him help? He held me so tight as we looked into each other's eyes and he told me how much he loved me and that he wasn't going to make it and he didn't want to make it. He has always said that if he couldn't walk or be his independent self he didn't want to live. He loved me more than anything in this world and he wouldn't change one thing about his life and he didn't want to even think about leaving the boys, but it is what it is and there isn't anything any of us can do about it.

From the moment we found out he had cancer at 28 I feared that I had brought this on him, my bad luck from my life. I had always thought my dad was 29 when he died and I feared every moment of my life that something would happen to Brett at 29. So in this conversation he promised me that he would do everything he could to hold on until 30 so I didn't feel like I had done this to him. He was so worried about taking care of me and us that he never worried about dying and what that would mean for him. That night we fell asleep in each other's arms, knowing that the end was near and there wasn't anything we could do about it but love each other every moment that we could. About 2:30 that morning I woke up to Brett gasping for breath. I sat up straight and tried to wake him thinking he was having another bad dream, when he wasn't waking I got to the light and as I turned it on he started to have a grand mal seizure.

Our children were in the other room sound asleep and my husband was helplessly seizing with no end in sight. I called 911 and cried hysterically for Brett's attention and for him to come back to me. The 15 minutes alone with him waiting for the paramedics to arrive were probably the longest of my life. His blank stare at the ceiling following the seizing sent me over the edge and the paramedics found me on his chest crying and listening to his breathing trying to get him to come out of it and respond to me. By the time we reached the hospital Brett was starting to come around and I described to him what happened and where he was and that I loved him. His family was there immediately and we all just prayed and prayed with everything we had. While we were waiting to be transfers to University of Pennsylvania where his doctors were Brett had another seizure, which I was alone for yet again. This time he didn't come back to me. We spent 5 days at the hospital, countless tests, countless doctors coming over and over to tell me he isn't coming back from this there is nothing I can do and hospice is now our only option.

Chapter 7: Testimony

I lay in his hospital bed with him at night every night to keep him calm and remind him that the nurses are there and help and where he is. If I was handed one more grief packet or counseling service card I think I was going to throw myself off the roof. I wanted my husband back, I wanted him to hold me and be the strong one and tell me everything was going to be ok. We were finally cleared to come home on Friday evening, Brett still didn't really know where he was and what had happened but as the doctors said they had him on anti-seizure medicine and the disease was now so bad in his brain there was nothing else they could do for him. As we lay in bed Friday night he tried to get out, he was disoriented, didn't know where he was and was very upset and confused.

It was almost like a light switch came on Saturday morning. The kids were in the living room watching TV, and I had come in to get Brett up and bring him his breakfast in bed. He looked at me like he knew who I was and pulled me down on the bed. He held me and looked into my eyes and asked me what happened to him. I swear, I can't describe the clarity he seemed to have like nothing ever happened, like I had him back for a brief shining moment. I asked him what he remembered and he said not much and I had to relive the last week and every conversation the doctors had with us. I had to look the love of my life in the eyes and tell him he was going to die. No one should ever have to do that or feel that or hear that. He said ok, held me while I cried and told me he wanted to go back to sleep, he was really tired. From that moment on, Brett gave up. Each day became harder to wake him, and harder for him to want to eat or get out of bed. By Monday, a visit with the home health nurse and Brett refusing to help me lift him out of bed prompted me to finally call hospice. I refused to make the call before because making that call meant I was giving up on my husband. After I spoke to the nurse she promised me that all that call means is that we get more help to make Brett more comfortable. So I called and made an appointment for him to be enrolled in the program Tuesday morning. By Monday night Brett had really given up, he was tired and we snuggled in his chair all day. He would eat fruit as I fed it to him but not seeming interested in really wanting to eat.

Monday began the end. While his mom was dropping off one of our kids, Brett had another mild seizure to which he couldn't really talk afterwards and seemed to be in pain. Hospice was called and we were transferred to the hospice center than evening.

The Beginning of the End

Sitting in his chair with him waiting for the hospice nurse to show up Monday evening was the most difficult decision of my life. But what do you do? The doctors have told us there is nothing they can do. So do you go to the hospital and they poke and prod him or call hospice and they make him comfortable. How did we get here? How can this really be happening? This was not supposed to happen. We were supposed to get our miracle. Brett was supposed to be ok. The hospice nurse informed us that he was in pain and that we could either keep him home and let him continue to be in pain or take him to the center where they can control his pain.

I will never forget the ride there. In the back of the ambulance, holding his hand and trying to keep him calm, all while I know that it is only a matter of time that I will never be able to hold his hand again. I am going to lose him and he isn't going to come home. How does a person deal with that? How do you continue to hold that person knowing that your time is limited? How can any human endure watching the person they love die, knowing that death is so final and so real. I laid in bed with Brett watching him wither away peacefully moving to the Lord. Listening to his breathing, feeling him hold me close knowing that any breath could be our last together. The doctors and nurses couldn't give us a timeline, it could be hours to weeks because Brett's body was so young and strong. He was the 3rd youngest person to ever be admitted to that center. Nobody could help us and all we could do was wait to lose him.

On Wednesday evening his breathing changed and was a sure sign that things could be changing. They called his whole family to come back and as we all gathered around his bed, me sitting by his side he woke up and looked at me. I lost it, I was crying hysterically. I thought I was ready to let him go, I thought I wanted him to not suffer anymore but when the time was actually near I couldn't imagine losing him. I cried please don't leave me. Please don't leave me! He looked at me with confusion and grabbed hastily at a pillow lying next to him. He wasn't speaking much so I asked if he was uncomfortable and wanted a pillow. He shook his head violently and pulled at the pillow again. I asked if he wanted the pillowcase. He shook his head yes and I pulled the pillow out threw it across the room and gave him the case. He pulled my shirt down so I was right in front of his face and pulled at the pillowcase. I honestly for a split second thought maybe I had hurt his head with all my crying and he was going to put the case over my head. But he didn't, in front of all of our family he balled up the pillowcase and wiped my tears with it. Then he laid me down next to him and smoothed the pillowcase out over top of me like a blanket. He then motioned with his finger for everyone to come closer and he uttered the words in a whisper, "Take care of her."

It took 5 more days for Brett's body to finally give into the cancer. He died two days before Christmas. My life, our lives have never be the same and I don't think they ever will.

Finding Strength

I am not going to write this book and pretend that I am the strongest person in the world that can get through anything. I am a person, a person that is insecure, who cries, who bleeds, who questions, who has fears and worries. But I am going to tell you how this journey has brought me closer to God and has allowed me to trust in His plan. There are some lessons in life you just wish you didn't have to learn the hard way. Don't get me wrong it always helps you to learn them but one of them is how crazy things are after you lose a loved one.

Brett was literally my whole world. For 13 years we made every decision together, I relied on his thoughts of me to drive every action and decision I ever made. I alone watched him take his last breath and that is a moment you can never describe that will change the person you are to the core. Other people can tell you that they have lost someone close to them or a family member but to watch your other half, the person you vowed to spend the rest of your life with and become joined together in life take their final breath with, will cut you to your core. Some might call me damaged, I guess so, but I am pretty sure I was plenty damaged before. It is because of that damage, that pain and severe life altering loss that I am able to sit here today and write this. I am strong. They don't give you classes in school on what happens in life. We all know that death is a part of life but they don't tell you the process that you have to go through not only emotionally after losing someone you love but also everything else that goes into place.

Fifteen minutes after we lost him the decisions began, what funeral home do you want to call? What time can you be there tomorrow to make arrangements? What flowers do you want? Where do you want to be buried? How many plots do you want? Mind you, we lost Brett two days before Christmas, made arrangements and picked out burial plots on Christmas eve and I had to do Santa for our now 4 and 2 year old that evening, without Brett. That gives you no time, no time to realize what has happened, no time to realize that person that just was taken out of your life, no time to realize that your life will never be the same. It has been a journey to say the least the past 3 months. I can honestly say, as I am sitting here right now I have experienced every emotion under the sun known to man except anger, maybe that will come later. I'm told grief really doesn't have stages, I'm told everyone is different, I 'm told who knows how I'll respond. In all of this I have never, not once got angry at God. God doesn't give people cancer to test us; He loves us. Is cancer a part of our lives because of our lifestyles and the changes in our lifestyles over the past several hundred years, I think so, but who am I? I know that God didn't give Brett cancer. As I sit here today and profess my love for the Lord and my trust in His plan I can tell you how I came to that faith.

Three days after I lost Brett, it was the day after Christmas, which I am sure you can imagine, was probably one of the most difficult experiences of my life to have Christmas morning without daddy. I had to make a trip to Dover to get ready for services and shop for an outfit to wear. Yet another experience no one tells you about, shopping for what you are wearing to your husband's funeral. I had lunch with my mother in law and we were talking about her tattoo that she got for Brett and his sister when they were diagnosed with melanoma. And yes, I said they.

After Brett was diagnosed, everyone in his family was checked by the dermatologist and they found a stage one mole on his sister's ankle. He absolutely saved her life. Brett's Mom and I were talking about her tattoo and I commented that I always wanted one and never had anything meaningful enough to put on my body forever. I left lunch and thought about it some more and decided I wanted Brett with me always, no matter what happened in my life, who I met or where I went I never wanted to forget the person that he was, the person that I loved, the person I gave my life to. I had a friend in high school that I had heard was a local tattoo artist and after visiting several parlors I found him.

As I walked through the door his jaw hit the floor and asked how I had been since we hadn't seen each other in almost 10 years. I started hysterically crying, told him why I was there and begged him to give me a tattoo for Brett. In my emotional state I had no idea that there was a process involved in getting a tattoo, which included appointments, sketches and time to make sure this is really what you wanted to do. I didn't have time for all that, I wanted it and I needed it. He said he would if I took the afternoon and thought about it some more and had a clear idea of what I wanted to get. I am telling you this story because it was literally the first moment I thought about God after Brett and it happened in the middle of a busy mall. I did as he said and took the time, I ran my errands and went to the mall to find the outfits I was dreading buying. In the midst of the chaos, everyone running around joyfully spending their Christmas money, I was there to by shoes and a shirt to wear to my husband's funeral drowning in the thought of what tattoo I may want and if I really want to do it. In the dressing room I sat down for a few minutes. I cried and thought about what I was doing there, what I am I going to do with my life and I took out my phone and decided right then I was going to take control. I was getting a tattoo.

I started to Google tattoos and it hit me literally like a ton of bricks. I remembered a melanoma blog I had read over the summer while doing my research. A girl's sister had melanoma and she got the most beautiful tattoo on her shoulder blade that read, "I believe in miracles." That instantly struck a chord with me and for one brief moment I actually had allowed myself to think about God and what that phrase meant to me and I literally said out loud, "well I can't do that because I don't believe in miracles. I didn't get mine."

It took me that second to question Gods power to realize how stupid I was for even thinking that. My thought immediately went to Brett; his perspective on his entire journey through life, "it is what it is." God didn't do this to him, he wasn't going to zap him and make him all better, and all this was part of the plan. I don't have to like the plan or understand it but it was part of the plan. Then I realized as if it was there all along, Brett was my miracle. He was sent into my life for a reason. He saved my life, he gave me strength and love and trust and the family that I needed and a reason to live and love. He was my miracle. How could I possibly deny God's love for me when He allowed me to have such an amazing, life changing person in my life, even if it wasn't for as long as I wanted? I got my tattoo as a daily reminder that God doesn't always give you what you want, what I wanted was my life back, what I wanted was Brett to be happy and healthy and us to grow old together on the front porch and watch our children grow. But that wasn't part of the plan. As the weeks wore on I grew closer and closer to God.

The Power of the Plan

How can one person even describe the amount of emotions they feel in the grieving process? If I were to try to write even about one day, you would think I had multiple personalities and commit me here and now. The emotions and feelings are literally on a minute-by-minute basis. One minute I feel at peace because I had closure with the way he left me and how sick he was, the next minute I a fearful of being alone, cut to five minutes later I just want someone to hold me and tell me it's going to be ok. I am notorious for craving the physical touch to the point where I would say I'd take a hug from a stranger right now.

I think the emotions are even more complicated by the fact that I lost him to cancer and how he lost himself before we ever lost him physically, add to that the fact that we are young, we did think we were invincible and now I am a single mom with two little boys who daddy was their hero. When people tell me they have no idea how I feel, well I just nod and say no you don't. It makes it almost laughable when people try to put themselves in your shoes and make judgments on the feelings and actions you have because let's be honest, I don't even understand how I feel so how could they possibly begin to try.

My past has been an asset and a deterrent in coping with the overwhelming situation of losing the most amazing person I've ever met. An asset because this isn't my first round with life being unfair. I knew life could hand you situations like this my whole life, I actually fear this. I also know that it could be so much worse. One of my biggest pet peeves is when people look at me in pity like my life is so horrible. I want to wake them up and say do you see all the blessings that God gives my children and me every day? Do you know how many people out there have so much harder of a life and experiences? Trust me, this is awful and I wouldn't wish it on my worst enemy but couldn't life always be worse?

Brett's death made me mistrust everyone, I have lost the one person in my life I had finally let it. I had trusted Brett to love me and care for me and always be there and by losing him, I lost trust. It is very hard to grieve and depend on others when you feel like you can trust them to not hurt you, and at this point in life I am fairly certain I am at my maximum of the hurt threshold. I have been trying to go at this alone. Doing that I realized that there is someone I can trust, I can trust God. Now I am not going to lie to you and say magically overnight I was saved and instantly feel better and the world is a bright and shiny place again. I can tell you that because of my prayer and constant turning to Him, He put people in my life and peace in my life that have forever changed me.

Everyone has a Purpose

Do you ever wonder what your purpose is? I do all the time and I don't think we are supposed to know our purpose. I think that we will look back and realize as we go through God's plan what our purpose was. So as I prayed for peace and help and strength to get through this I met some people that had a purpose in my life. I'll tell you the story and you can decide for yourself if you think God has a plan.

About 6 years ago, back when Brett and I were struggling through those years after high school, finding ourselves, newly married, creating a life that seemed would never get started we finally had the chicken houses built. One of the servicemen for our chicken houses was named Joe. Now let me preface this story by saying that Brett wasn't fond of service people. He grew up in the chicken industry and the service people were usually big shots that had never grown a chicken who try to tell you what to do, according to Brett.

Brett was going on and on about this young guy who was close to our age that was his new service person. Brett really liked him, so much so that he introduced me to Joe. I have to tell you that I don't remember that meeting, but I know that it happened. Joe, in a completely side note conversation asked Brett if he had life insurance. Joe being faith filled seemed to have some reason to share that with Brett. Brett was 24 at the time and I was 23, pregnant with our second child. Joe mentioned to Brett that his father sold life insurance and he was from Alabama. Well long story short, a few short months later Mr. Don from Alabama was sitting at our kitchen table. We didn't get much but Brett trusted this person and signed up for a policy for him and me and planned on paying the policy for the rest of our lives.

I thought it sounded a little too good to be true and life had taught me that people really weren't that nice, there had to be a catch. Needless to say 4 years later Brett was diagnosed with Melanoma I had to talk to Mr. Don again for the first time since getting life insurance. I called him 2 weeks after Christmas. Words cannot describe to you the person I found on the other end of the phone. Compassionate, faith filled and caring. Mr. Don wears many hats, insurance guru, financially savvy, father, husband and pastor. He took the time to come up and deliver the policy personally and visited me several other times out of the kindness of his heart to check on me or called me to just check in. God puts people in your life for a reason. In all of my conversations with Mr. Don you can hear the passion he has for his family, and his kids are no exceptions. I had met one of them once, and heard Brett talk about him a lot and that was Joe. Don talked about Joe with such amazing regard all the time and it just brought a smile to my face to realize that some parents really do love their children unconditionally.

In one conversation he had mentioned that he told Joe about Brett and that Joe would probably be calling or texting me about it soon. I got the text that I had really gotten from everyone else, "Hi Sam, you don't know me but I am very sorry to hear about Brett and if you ever need anything at all I am here." I answered with my standard thank you so much I really appreciate it and never gave another thought about it.

As the weeks went on, I got a text once a week from our friendly ex-service man from Mississippi with an amazing scripture and thoughtful words just checking in. To be honest looking back I was completely confused how someone could be so kind and caring to a complete stranger and continue to pray and uplift a person they weren't going to get anything from. Then it came time for me to make the decision to leave teaching and take over the family farm or leave the farm.

I chose to follow Brett's dream and keep the farm going for our children to one day inherit what their daddy dreamt of building for them. By far one of the most eye opening and painful moments in the grieving process because it was real, my life had really changed, he really wasn't here anymore, I had been so strong through this so tough and I couldn't avoid it anymore. I laid on the floor to our family room and cried for a day and a half and I didn't want to reach out because I had no one to reach out to. The people that could understand were grieving too; they couldn't help me when they were feeling the same hopelessness. So I reached out to Joe, I will never forget that moment, the moment I asked a complete stranger for a scripture to get me through the day. As I lay on the floor sobbing my phone continues to signal text message after text message. Scripture after scripture like he had them all on the tip of his tongue, all-pertinent to helping me and I instantly felt peace.

I knew in that moment on that floor that the only person that can give me the peace I need is God. People cannot possibly describe to you the moment they give their life to the Lord and have you feel it but I can tell you that it is an indescribable feeling to feel the peace that scripture can give you. I will never doubt that this was part of the plan, that Brett met Joe all those years ago and I found Joe who helped me find peace in God. Everyone asks the question, "How do you know you are on the path God has for you?" I don't really know the answer to that and I am honestly not going to pretend like I know every scripture and every verse to try to answer that.

What I can tell you is my story and how I know. I realized for the first time in my life I don't have control, we don't have control of our plan. Sure we can control our actions and make choices for ourselves but if it is God's will it will happen. I truly believe that He will give you signs and put people in your lives for a reason to help guide you to that plan. For example, a recent decision that I made that seemed completely and utterly crazy to other people, I did it anyway and in my journey I happened to sit next to a woman on a plane. She saw my tattoo asked about it and I ended up telling her my whole life story and about my faith in God and His plan for my life and how much peace I have knowing that no matter what there is a plan for me and this will all work out. She looked at me with tears in her eyes and said to me that she thinks that God put me in her life to remind her to trust Him because she has been struggling with her faith recently and she prayed for answers.

To me, I don't know how anyone else would take that, but I feel as those that is one of those moments when God reassured me I was on the right path. The thing about moments is you have to be quiet, open, reflective and trusting enough to recognize them. People have commented to me recently about my outlook on life and how they don't know how I am doing it. I reply with Christ. Honestly, I don't know how people do it without Him. He gives you exactly what you need, not necessarily what you want. He has put people in my life that will forever leave a mark, Mr. Don with his wisdom, love and compassion, Joe with his faith and friendship, Ms. Gina (Mr. Don's wife) who I am fairly certain is my twin in another time and who cares about me and has never met me for a moment of her life, my church congregation that I have sat next to for years and never really allowed myself to open up to. All of these people have been given to me by God to renew my faith in people and faith in his plan for me.

My journey is just beginning, and it isn't unlike many other people. I am not special, or unique or talented, but I am blessed to have the Lord in my life and to have the peace he has given me. I am excited about what the next chapters to this tale have in store. They may not always be joyous and I am mature enough to know that there are still many hard times ahead but I am blessed in knowing that no matter what I face I don't face it alone. For nothing else I want this book to be a reminder that no matter how large our problems seem, we can't face them alone, and I cannot imagine not sharing my experience with the Lord with others. We live on a farm and the only way I can describe the way I feel about sharing the peace he gives me is this. If you watch all of your friends in the field picking corn by hand for 18 hours a day in the heat with health ailments and struggles and you know of a program that provides combines for free wouldn't you tell them about it? I certainly would share that information that could change their lives and set them free from struggling. Isn't that what God does for us? He doesn't take away the struggles but He certainly helps you through them. I wish anyone who reads this blessings and peace from the Lord and only ask that you share your story with someone and one by one we can all make a difference in this world. It only takes one kind smile, word, testimony, or role model to change the world. I hope that I can be a part of that change and I know everyone around me can as well. God Bless.

Samantha Gustafson

A Testimony by a Strong Woman

(This testimony is by one of the greatest people in my life. She is my sister, my strength, my supporter and my best friend. Her journey with the Lord has inspired me and brought me to tears. I am so thankful that she allowed the Lord into her life and also allowed me to be a part of that journey. Her testimony is so powerful and my hope and prayer is that reading her testimony can inspire someone to come to the Lord and seek his refuge, strength, guidance and wisdom.)

What am I doing here? Sitting in my car, outside of my sister's house, staring into the garage. Why did I choose to come all the way out here when I could be at home; on the couch; eating quick dinner; and releasing all of work's tension and stress into a marathon of Real Housewives of Where-ever? Make no mistake; this is a choice to be here. I have chosen to give up comfort, (literally, I'm still in my binding work clothes) and not to feed my now growling belly.

I think I've known for a while now that something is missing. All this time I believe that what is missing is something that I can achieve myself. That happiness lies at the end of a journey, it lies with a certificate that states I am admitted to a Bar that I've held in such high esteem my entire life, and standing in the Supreme Court, swearing to uphold and defend the Constitution of the United States and the Constitution of the State of Delaware. But that achievement…that perceived happiness is now at least another year away. Even thought despair and defeat (that I feel every waking moment of my life), I am not satisfied to resign myself to be unhappy for another year. I may know very little about my spirituality and my relationship with God, but I know that He does not want me to be unhappy, and every moment I spend unsatisfied with myself, is a moment wasted, and a moment that I am rejecting His glory in me, His path for me, His love for me.

I've tried to pass that exam. Maybe I haven't tried hard enough but that doesn't mean I will stop trying. Each year is a new opportunity (of which I am very grateful) to attempt to succeed and reach this goal that I hope will bring me happiness. I am left wondering on how to be successful this time around. What can I do differently? Is this it? A weekly Women's Bible Study with my sister, and her friends and family, some of which are acquaintances. What can these women do for me? What can I do for these women? What can God do for me? What can I do for God?

Something is missing. Maybe someone is missing. I have always helped myself to believe that I have a very individualized relationship with God. He knows who I am. He created me. With every flaw, strength, quirk, and eccentricity.

Do I know Him? Has my life suffered because I do not know Him? Is my life suffering? I could create a list, tallies of each side, of how I have prospered and how I have failed. I am not arrogant. I know that all of my achievements were not my sole doing. I mean, I did a lot of the work, but every opportunity, every instance of genius, every moment in which the Universe and God himself conspired to help me get to where I needed/wanted to be couldn't have been done only by me. Have I thanked Him? Have I given my glory to Him and used His divine inspiration to help His people? To even help myself?

As I sit here, I can't confidently answer my questions; why I'm here, for answers. My whole life I've taken tests. Test for placement into the public school system, every chapter in grade school, into the gifted program, into high school courses, SAT'S, DSTP'S, college placement, for my undergraduate degrees, LSAT'S, law school finals, and 2 Bar exams. I know how to answer questions. Even if I do not recall the answers, I can always make an educated guess. I know how to seek out what the test writer is really asking. I am having trouble finding answers to my questions. I need answers. I need to know what I am missing. I am no longer a runner, sprinting down a path, and questioning everything that comes along. This is a new role for me. This is the plan He has laid at my feet.

I come to Him, humbly, a little ashamed for all of my past transgressions. Though, I do not worry if He will accept me. His unconditional love is something I learned very early on... "Jesus loves me, this I know...." SING WITH ME NOW! I know that my relationship with Him can be so much more and I do not expect to be rewarded simply for seeking a renewed relationship... that a close relationship to God is a prize to be won. Rather, through a closer relationship with God I may achieve those aspirations, and if not, it is because He has something greater for me. I mean, I hope He designs to bless me with this achievement, but we'll cross that bridge when we come to it.

So, again, what am I doing here? I have questions, plenty of them. I thought I would be getting all the answers. At least, I thought I needed all the answers. Maybe not but point is not having my questions answered, but to keep asking questions. Keep talking to God. Lay my burdens at His feet, because to carry them the way I have been would be to stray from the path He has presented to me. Maybe the point is not to reach a destination, a line in the sand, a goal at the end of a list but rather, to pay attention along the journey. Look up to Him for guidance when I feel lost, and take happiness in the ability to keep moving. Only through His grace is this possible.

I guess I can now stop asking, "What am I doing here?" And start saying, "HERE I AM, LORD!" I hope you are ready for me, because I am ready for you. I pray that you come to my life and use me as a vessel for your will. Through your grace, I can achieve, I can rise up to meet my destiny, your plan for me, and I can become the woman, attorney, the friend, the lover, the mother, the daughter, the sister, the seeker, the giver, and the leader you have blessed me to be. AMEN.

A Testimony by Concerned Mother

(This testimony is written by one of the strongest and most loving woman I know. She has always been there for me and continues to be my rock in trials and successes. The strength it took to not only let the Lord in to help in the trial she faced but to also be brave enough to share it with others to help even one other person is astounding. I am so thankful that God always sends people into my life to show his power and glory and this person is one of those lights. As you read her testimony, allow the holy spirit to stir within you an awakening of life and power that he lives in you.)

I got married young, had 3 beautiful, healthy children. We have a nice home, decent jobs, and we work at having a good marriage, not great, not perfect, but overcome many mistakes we continue to make. We appreciate the life we have. I thought we were pretty lucky.

Children grew more beautiful; all 3 graduated high school with honors. Our oldest two went to college, earned bachelor and master's degrees; our youngest was less interested in education but made a go. I thought that was the most important thing to teach them, to become successful and happy; what was needed I thought, was education. I thought that was the necessary tool. I had not achieved that tool, so I thought the void I had was furthering my education. I made the youngest pick any school, 4 year school, tech school, University or community college, just had to make a decision.

The school was 6 hours away but I thought, it would take going away to school to grow up and make better decisions. Seeing the school the first time my feeling was this is not the right fit for my child, but was convinced it was the thought of losing my baby even though the feeling was to the point of physical sickness, I pushed it aside. I spoke to my kids daily most often everything seemed pretty great until maybe around October 2007.

Thanksgiving 2007 came and my child was different. The happy, fun loving, generous, kind, caring person seemed withdrawn and distant not eager for family holiday dinners that were once so cherished by all my children. My child went through the motions but something was wrong. The smile was missing, the laughter was taken away. Trouble sleeping, concentrating at school, participating in family fun became issues. I remember asking where a favorite winter coat was since they did not wear it off the plane. That went unanswered for a month or so. December 2007 my child calls me; barely recognizing the voice in horror, a voice full of fear under the cry, like I have never heard, and a sound I have never known, a pain I never knew possible to feel.

I drove six hours in the middle of the night nonstop to the mountains and in heavy snow; the drive was what felt like a lifelong horrible dream, awake and in a living nightmare. When finally arriving I saw my then 17 almost 18 year old soaked, shivering, scared and hiding by a dumpster waiting for me in the cold snow for hours. I tried to get my child to talk about what was going on but was not successful. I began looking though the bags of personal belongings that I picked up from the school, and found the missing winter coat, and an ID badge for school. The coat was stained in blood one sleeve had the largest amount of blood and looked like it was used for wiping a face or nose. The nametag was mangled somehow. I knew it was darker than bullying; uglier than a fistfight. I thought my mind; soul and heart were forever broken. I asked but got no real answers. Drugs became involved. I did what I could and thought what was best; I called the school, police, lawyers, doctors and more doctors. Some were known as the best therapist. Family and private sessions followed and my husband attended one family session and refused to go back. The doctors prescribed depression medication and then it turned horribly wrong.

My picture perfect family life was no more, everything changed, relationships, my thoughts, state of mind, appearance, even my body changed. I thought all for the worse. I have always had a good family and a great circle of supportive friends but nothing was getting better. I felt alone. I put on a face to function at work and in the public at home I often showered for private breakdowns and tried to function normally.

I started watching Joel Osteen often and seemed to find brief comfort. I encouraged all my children to start watching him, I would call them, text them and let them know when he was on. Sometimes they would watch but maybe never, they did not share my enthusiasm. Often I watched alone and often my youngest was in another room of the house. I thought he never listened at all.

Over a year closer to two years of everything becoming devastatingly worse, self-destructing... doctors letting me know that with the trauma assault (only thing I was told) that they believed happened to my child and my child self-medicating with drugs that the suicide rate was 85% for my child. Fear was my everyday, fear and guilt took over my life. I thought someone had to tell me everything, what was wrong, what happened, I thought I had to know the why, what, I thought I deserved to know! I thought it would make is better... bearable.

Finally, for some unknown reason to me, changes started to take place in my child, for seconds I noticed a smile...soon minutes, and soon even days, if I actually heard the sound of his laughter it brought tears of joy to my face. He had started going to church, reading the Bible and sharing hope with the family. This change was hard for us to grasp we seldom attended church. Many family members were not open to the mention of Jesus and did not feel comfortable. They blamed the Church. A few family members referred to the church as a cult. They were uncomfortable and treated my adult child cruelly and often physically. After seeing these changes I went to this church to see if this was a source of hope and inspiration and the will to live; my child was showing signs of even if others did not see it as a positive thing.

I still was consumed by worry inside myself. I continued to be afraid and silently not know where my adult child was at every second and if this would be the last time I saw them, was not my life. I thought my burden alone to keep. I went to church more often and when singing praises to the Lord I would find myself crying, listening to the message; I would cry and even though it was in the pew where less people sat and I thought well hidden, I could not control the tears that over took my face every Sunday for almost 2 hours.

One Sunday a lady with long silver hair, that sat at the other end of the long mostly empty pew was suddenly right next to me and while we were singing praises to God she placed one of her hands on my shoulder and softly began praying over me, I normally would have found it impossible to hear someone in a church full of people singing. She spoke some of the same words I heard in church but never grasped, I was moved by them. I heard her differently that Sunday for some reason; she was praying for me, she was praying that I would give this to him. That I would find comfort in Jesus and everything started feeling different inside. I am not sure of the date or anything else that day in church, not sure who did the message, not sure of a single word spoke to me, not sue how I drove home with eyes that were just a pool of pain, and my mind, I thought I actually may have already lost my mind completely. The feelings and overcoming emotions were chaos.

The next thing I do remember was being on my knees with my arms raised towards the ceiling in my bedroom floor and saying words that in previous months; I thought only other people would ever say. I never thought could be a reality for me. I asked for my child to want to live, I did not need to know what or when, did not have to know the details in the past any longer, I have them up, I surrendered. I surrendered that day in my bedroom floor… and I never thought the same and now I believe because the Bible tells me so and in the Bible I found Peace.

"Come unto me, all who are weary and burdened, and I will give you rest." Matthew 11:28

"I can do all things through Christ who strengthens me" Philippians 4:13

"Be Joyful in Hope, Patient in affliction and Faithful in prayer" Romans 12:12

Everyday is a gift, everyday can test us, everyday is new, everyday we have a choice to be kind, encouraging and mostly grateful. Everyday is possible. All the Glory to GOD. My son changed, not back to who he was before, but brand new in late 2009. He is a kind, fun loving, hardworking, generous young man and a divorced single great dad blessed with 2 angels. Later I learned my child's changes started one night in a fetal position on the bathroom floor, trying to leave this world; but then at the exact right time (God's timing) he heard me watching Joel Osteen and the prayer at the end of every broadcast his ministry offers spoke to him.

I pray this gives a mother direction and peace.

Samantha Gustafson

Chapter 8

More Praise than Doubt

As I begin to write this chapter I am brought back to the beginning of this adventure. I have always loved to write and it has been a great outlet for me. I have started several fiction stories that have never been completed because I never knew how they were going to end. Then the Lord spoke to me about this book. He literally handed me in a whisper the titles of each of the chapters. I wrote them down immediately (because I learned to do this while I was on fire and immediately heard from the Lord) or else I would forget the urgency in the message. As I wrote them down I had no idea the content that I would write about and what scriptures would be inside. However, at the beginning of each writing session I pray and it always seems that life brings me right back to my writing. Which is pretty amazing. You are literally reading my journey with the Lord, my walk through life. This is a living breathing testimony to His amazing and steadfast love for each one of us.

As I write it still amazes me how He carries us through situations and in hindsight we realize exactly why we went through what we did, well most of the time. This time, my trouble led me to this chapter and as I opened my notebook to see what the next chapter title was to be, I literally chuckled to myself and to the Lord thinking how appropriate this content would be in this moment in my life. More praise than doubt, what a novel concept. Sure when I was in my peak and fully relying on God and spending all of my heartbroken time building strength in Him and fully engulfed with being on fire I had praise that was unimaginable. Has anyone out there let life, or maybe the enemy slip in and steal that praise? I thought I was invincible with my fervent faith and my relationship with the Lord. He had brought me through so much and so much yet to come. Losing my husband and the life I was faced with after has been one of the greatest challenges I have ever had to face, but the Lord was able to bring me through that, worshiping and praising all the while. And then it hit. Real life, you know when you have reached that appropriate amount of time after tragedy (and I have yet to figure out what that means) when you go back to life. Maybe not life as you knew it but a new life. A life that sometimes is uncomfortable, that hurts and robs us of joy and comfort and safety. I am in that moment. Where I know my word enough to know that he will never leave or forsake me and the gift of the Holy Spirit is ever present within me, but the doubt and the fear and anxiety come creeping in ever so slowly almost so slowly that they have taken over before you even knew it was there.

That is me now. I was doing wonderful, worshiping, holding steadfast to the promises the Lord has made me and you. Every day I repeat Jeremiah 29:11. Over and over in my head I repeat He has a plan for me and I am going to prosper. So then how, in my worship, my reading, my Bible study and my love for God did I allow for doubt and fear to enter my world and begin stealing my joy? How could I let that happen? I know better. I know the tactics of the enemy. I know what he uses, I throw scripture in his face and stomp out his power and yet, here I am sitting, losing hope, filling with fear, anxiety and even doubting my worth as a person.

The second that I let those thoughts in and entertained the idea I started to lose my praises. Not that I didn't have plenty to praise for. Trust me, my life is beyond blessed, I have a roof over my children and my heads, a wonderful family and a great support system, blessed I tell you. I began to find that I had lost the joy that I was so used to carrying. The light, that seemed to shine when others seemed dull around me was now gone. I lost the spark that kept telling me that is going to be ok and there was going to be a plan. It didn't happen all at once, I allowed it to happen. I let the stresses of life and learning how to live it alone, physically of course not spiritually. The emotional rollercoaster that is going from being married to a widow with two small children trying to tackle dating, relationships or even just learning how to survive. I am sure that many people can relate to the feelings of the emotional spiritual rollercoaster. Being on fire one minute and letting feelings take you in a different direction. Then I realized that I am human. God knew who He created and that I am special, worth it and valued to Him. I would tell myself this all the time, pray and really hold onto those words of comfort and yet I still felt the hope draining out of me like a slow leak and I felt powerless to stop it. I knew it was happening and every day I felt like I was fighting so hard to hold onto that hope, that life giving raft that God had thrown me when he showed me the way but it was slipping away from me as I was slipping into more feelings of being lost, lonely and unworthy of love.

Then after a difficult night tonight, I pray one last time, and ask God for what seems like the 84 thousandth time to take my hand and guide me through this day and give me strength and it seemed like I had the strength all along. I realized that I have to surround myself with encouragers, people that aren't going to look at me like I am crazy and recognize what is happening to me as an attack to interrupt the work God has laid before me. A plan to put me so far down emotionally I wouldn't even want to look up anymore because I wouldn't feel worthy, I wouldn't feel worth it, and honestly I was so beaten up inside I was physically tired of trying to fight it. In that moment of constantly keeping myself surrounded by people that encouraged me to keep looking up, and not in the keep your chin up kind of way (those people really irritate me), but in the you know your God and you have faith in His plan kind of way. Instead of wallowing tonight I opened my book and I felt refreshed to continue His work and share the struggles of everyday and how with God anything is possible. The lowest of low, the most defeated and down trodden situation can be handled and manipulated by God to bring Him glory and you peace. Now I am not saying it's going to be easy, or even fun but He is our creator and all good comes from Him.

As I opened my notebook a scripture was written Psalms 86:15 "But you, O Lord, are a God merciful and gracious, slow to anger and abounding in steadfast love and faithfulness." How amazingly comforting is that knowing that He is always there with steadfast love and faithfulness. Not roller coaster love like we are used to. Honey I'm happy with you right now because you brought me flowers love and then I'm mad at you now because you didn't take the trash out kind of love. God's love is ever present and steadfast. The same today, tomorrow and yesterday, regardless of sin and situation.

I guess that takes me right back to the topic of this chapter and how it just fits so perfectly into my life, my night and well everything. I think people need to hear that we aren't perfect. I think we all really need to hear that it is ok to have emotions, it is ok to feel, it is ok to hurt and be angry or upset or joyous and overjoyed. Scripture even says it:

"A time to be born and a time to die, a time to plant and a time to uproot, a time to kill and a time to heal, a time to tear down and a time to build, a time to weep and a time to laugh, a time to mourn and a time to dance, a time to scatter stones and a time to gather them, a time to embrace and a time to refrain from embracing, a time to search and a time to give up, a time to tear and a time to mend, a time to be silent and a time to speak, a time to love and a time to hate, a time for war and a time for peace." Ecclesiastes 3: 2-8

God doesn't say to be joyous and singing all the days of our lives and always be happy. He states that there is a season for everything. I am in a season of mourning, I cannot expect myself to be happy all the time, or laugh and dance as though I'm happy. From how happy and safe I felt in the Lord I was trying to do just that. Be joyous and happy, dance and shout because that is what I thought it meant to love the Lord and be the person He designed me to be. He knows us better than we know ourselves. The Holy Spirit is there to intercede on our behalf when we just utterly have no clue. So why do we put this pressure on ourselves to associate praise with uncontrollable joy and slap on a smile to the outside world to proclaim that we are happy in all situations. I really thought that was what I was supposed to do, I really thought that it wasn't ok for me to be sad, that if I really loved the Lord and had faith in God my father that I shouldn't be sad because I know He has this. I know now that I can still praise God and mourn. I can still praise God, in my sadness and despair. Trust me, I don't want those feelings but they are there and partially to attack me and keep me down but most of them are just human emotions. It takes me to read, reflect and think about the love of our almighty Father to realize how much He really does love us and how well He knows His creation. He knew we would have moments of laughter and sadness, sowing and reaping and yet His love is steadfast though all those moments and His understanding and compassion is relentless.

So not only can I take a deep breath and finally rest in the fact that my weeping is no reflection on my love or faith in God and that my season is just that a season that God already knew was going to happen then I can open up to praise. We can't do this life alone. If you think you can than you are wrong and a fool. We need God, we need the Holy Spirit and we need faith. As much as you need Him, he is already there waiting to see you and I through it, but sometimes it takes encouragement. Maybe from a stranger, your hairdresser, your neighbor or a coworker, but God always sends the encouragement when you need it.

"Praise the Lord, my soul. I will praise the Lord all my life; I will sing praise to my God as long as I live. Do not put your trust in princes, in human beings, who

cannot save. When their spirit departs, they return to the ground; on the very day their plans come to nothing. Blessed are those whose help is the God of Jacob, whose hope is in the Lord their God. He is the Maker of Heaven and earth, the sea, and everything in them he remains faithful forever. He upholds the cause of the oppressed and gives food to the hungry, the Lord sets prisoners free, and Lord gives sight to the blind, the Lord lifts up those who are bowed down, the Lord loves the righteous. The Lord watches over the foreigner and sustains the fatherless and the widow, but he frustrates the ways of the wicked. The Lord reigns forever, your God, O Zion, for all generations. Praise the Lord". Psalms 146 1-10

One of my favorite scriptures that I need to be reminded of on a daily basis is James 1:2-4

"Consider it pure joy, my brothers and sisters, whenever you face trials of many kinds, because you know that the testing of your faith produces perseverance. Let perseverance finish its work so that you may be mature and complete, not lacking anything."

I love this scripture because it helps me to focus my lens a little more clearly on the Lord and not my present situation. It helps me to dial in that focus on what I should be praising for and not the fear and doubt or emotion I am experiencing. God knew we would all experience these moments, which is why He left us the ultimate guidebook to getting through them and arming myself with the word is the most powerful weapon I have.

So I praise, I praise in a thought because sometimes a thought is all I can get out, I praise in a whisper because sometimes I whisper is all I have left and then that whisper turns into an inside voice and then a shout and then a beautiful ballad of pure love. Accepting that struggle and emotions are a part of life and that it is ok to go through seasons and most importantly the closer I grown to God to realize His steadfast love I know that even my praise in thought is enough. He loves me and He knows my heart and that I long to praise and love Him. He knows my struggle as He knows yours and for me the victory to living every day is recognizing that I may get knocked down or beaten up but when I look up, I am looking to my father in praise and adoration and He is looking back at me with love.

Accepting that we are not perfect and understanding the greatness and glory of God's love is something to praise and if every day we strive to have just a few more thoughts of praise instead of doubt and worry than we are seeking the face of God and He will seek you back. You may feel like the lost lamb sometimes, well for me lately all the time but I know that He NEVER left a lamb behind and that I am loved beyond belief and my turning back to Him even if it's while laying face down on the ground in my lowest of low, that is my highest honor of praise, because I am telling my Lord that I still trust Him and love Him and praise His name on high to lift me up. So let's get the idealistic image out of our heads of the "perfect Christian" and stop letting the enemy in telling us if we aren't shouting like raving lunatics then we aren't praising. We praise God every moment we take that one step further in faith trusting in his unbounding love for us. I praise you Lord for brining me all of these steps and I praise you for all the steps you will continue to take me. Even if I can't always find the words to say it, I turn back to you in every moment because you are my God. Thank you.

So I close our chapter in prayer:

"God, please bless those who read and hear this and help give them peace and calm their fears, anxiety and doubts that creep into our daily lives. Please give them the deep seeded hope in the life you want for them and the love you have for them. Help them to see all the goodness you have before them and help them to recognize the moments of praise that they can give you. I speak for myself also Lord. Help us to always turn our face to you and praise you even in the struggles because we know those struggles are to complete us and make us lacking in nothing and when we can't see to find your face on our own, please God send us help so that we may praise

you for all that you deserve. In Jesus's great name I pray. Amen"

Samantha Gustafson

Chapter 9

You Are One, Together We Are Many, With God We Are Strong

I know I probably say this every chapter, but since I don't go back once the spirit has led me to write I can't say that for sure; however, God NEVER ceases to amaze me. I have said many times how this book came to be and the fact that I was led to write down the chapter headings months and months ago with no idea where my life would lead me and yet here I sit, working on the last chapter and because of my present circumstances God is having me fill this chapter.

Call me crazy but God is just so magnificent and all knowing. I know from scripture and digging into my word just how amazing God is, His love, His mercy, His grace, His forgiveness, but to actually witness His greatness, to have your eyes opened to the amazing things He works in our lives is just beyond my comprehension some days. This has been a very difficult year and a half to say the least. I have struggled, as you read earlier with everything from guilt to anger and frustration and every emotion in between. You name it and I have probably felt it at least twice on any given day. Yet here I sit, able to write, able to type my feelings about how great our God is. Now everyday isn't like this. Trust me, the past month and a half has been a doosey. I have been juggling how to be mom and dad, get back to what can only be called "normal life" again and you guessed it...trying to date. Grieving and moving forward are two opposite ideas that are seemingly impossible to do simultaneously but been interactively involved in my journey (unwillingly) I have met so many people. People that show me just how great God is and make me so thankful of His faithfulness and the friend that He always is.

People have been my lifeline, but not just any people, divine appointments as some call them. People that have been planted in the exact moment in my life to help me, show me or tell me what I need to get me moving forward. In all those interactions I realize that as I feel alone and isolated in my feelings of grief, like no one else in the whole world really understands my pain and the pain that rocks me every day when my kids ask why Daddy isn't coming home or I have to diffuse an argument between my 5 and 3 year old about what passing away is and why they will never see their Daddy until they get to heaven too. I realize that my pain really isn't that much different than so many other people I have met. We are all grieving something, and when I use the term grieve I mean we hold a sadness or have pain from some kind of loss or hurt that has shaped us and made us a tiny piece of the person that we are in that moment. I have done a lot of observing the past year and a half, which is new for me because I usually am doing more talking and entertaining than observing but what I have observed is the pain that we all carry with us every day. The feelings of inadequacy, loss, despair, hopelessness, anger, frustration, fear these are all debilitating aspects of pain that I have recognized and connected with so many people over. It always humbles me so much to listen or observe others and their pain and to realize we are really not that different. The Bible warns us in so many places of the pain and anguish that we will feel in this lifetime, and most of it is due to our own sin but some of it is to shape us into the people God intends us to become. What I have learned from listening to divorce stories, or loss, or maybe joblessness, or failing marriage is that in all of these situations people, even those with faith felt the same way I did, alone. They felt like nobody understood and if they did they couldn't help. They felt like their problems were so overwhelming and they were lost and on the brink of giving up hope.

It hits me so hard tonight to think and reflect on what all of these interactions has done to mold me into the woman I am right now, the woman that will be different and changed 5 months from now and again 5 years from now and so on because I want to continue to be changed and renewed by our Lord. Each of these people and their feelings and pain has brought me closer to God; to not only understand Him but to begin to really trust in Him for the path our life is supposed to take. Realizing that we aren't alone in our feelings is probably one of the most powerful tools we have as people and especially as Christians. God knew we would feel all of these things, why do you think he equipped us with a personal piece of Him to travel with us every day in the Holy Spirit. The Holy Spirit isn't a whisper of wind that blows past every once in a while when you need him, he is walking with you every single step you take, in the valley's and the peaks. He knows what God knows and he also feels your struggles and pain. What a reassuring feelings, what a comfort the great comforter provides.

I can only speak to myself in this text, because that is all I know and my journey will hopefully help and encourage at least one other person and that to me will be a success. However, most of the time I feel like one person, just little old me fighting through life. Now, I am trying to do that a little more successfully these days and arming myself with scriptures and knowledge, with prayer and obedience but I'm not the master designer or the master builder, I don't see myself in the great plan, I am just one person. Sometimes I feel like the most insignificant one person ever in history. I get down on myself with the inadequacy issues of not feeling worthy of others and worthy of my purpose and that makes me feel smaller than one, like I could disappear and people would actually be better off. I know that sounds a little morbid, but sometimes the truth hurts and God already knows when I have those feelings before I even speak them but the difference in those feelings I have now and before I was saved is I recognize those feelings for exactly what they are, an attack. An attack from the enemy, that knows and is scare of who lives in me. The enemy that wants so badly to bring every believer closer to the pit of despair, hopelessness, joblessness, fear, anxiety, loss, confusion, anger or hatred. He fears the good works that God is continuing to do in my life and yours and when I arm myself with the sword of God's word I can fight the attack because I see where it is coming from.

I tell you all this because this is me, the one, just one of millions and millions of people, insignificant, yet powerful and blessed. I feel so insignificant sometimes when I look at the news, watch politics and shake my head at the state of our world, what can I do? Jesus hurry and come back I say. Then I think about all the amazing times in only a year and a half since the veil has been lifted from my eyes that God has personally and miraculously worked in my life. Times that you couldn't deny Gods hand if you were the strongest willed atheist alive. God has really and truly worked on only my behalf to rescue me from a situation or save me from teetering any closer to the edge of that pit. How many times has he personally worked on your behalf? Even if you are new to your faith and can only count a handful think about that and put that in perspective to how amazing our God truly is and how we each are truly blessed, prized and irreplaceable to our Father. Is your mind blown? Because mine certainly is! We may be just one person, as we call ourselves. Just one single mom, just one dad, just one accountant, just one teacher, just one police officer, just one friend but God does NOT see us that way. He sees us as an interconnected and intertwined force of love and glory for him, which are loved, powerful and unbelievably blessed. To God we are not the insignificant one that we believe we are we are a powerful many.

I don't think I quite understood that concept until this very day. I am still very new in my walk. To me I say new, I have known God my whole life but to actually change and sacrifice my life to accept my Savior has been within the last two years and I am so thankful for all the work He still is yet to do in me and I praise him for that. But that being said, me being "new" as I call myself I am still very unaware of how I could be more than just the single mom and teacher in God's plan. Who am I? How could He possibly use me? I mean I see all the people that He uses around me to plant churches to be bold evangelist or to begin ministries but that's not me, I'm just the single mom trying to rely on my faith to survive another day in the hopes that I will find joy again. But today I realized Gods view of us, the view that once we accept Him and He begins His work in you, you are not the insignificant one that you imagine yourself to be, you are part of the powerful many.

Today as I was sitting in church, getting my fill of worship and renewing from the past week and praising for the week to come I felt so overwhelmingly grateful to be in the house of the Lord and in His immediate presence. You know those days when the Holy Spirit is just moving and you can almost feel it knocking you over as it plows through the crowd piercing hearts that seemed hard as rocks and bringing grown men to their knees to worship God. Well, today was one of those amazing days. Our worship was wonderful the message was inspiring and I always love when I feel like the pastor is speaking right to me and then it came time for the alter call. The message was about the missions God has us on in our personal lives on a daily basis and the choice we have to accept it and have faith that any mission God has you one, even the seemingly impossible ones are possible through God. As I mentioned in the beginning of the chapter the past month and a half have been a real struggle, life was getting the best of me and the pit that I had seen from a distance and teetered on the edge of to many times to count, I had found myself lying in the bottom of praying for a miracle for God to lift me out of. And He did, He never left my side, was it easy, no, it was miserable. I cried every day, was depressed and felt all of the feelings I mentioned before multiple times a day if not on a constant basis, but I held firm in Gods promises for me the individual and he saw me through it.

So as I walk to the alter today I want to just thank God for never leaving me in the pit and staying with me on the dark nights but also delivering me out of the pit stronger than when I fell in. I felt refreshed and ready to tackle the week as "the one" the individual, and the insignificant. And then it happened, I walked back to my seat and continued to praise God as others were being prayed over to the alter and I saw him. A young man standing at the alter looking a little lost. I had never seen him before, I am relatively new to this church, didn't know his story and his body language or look didn't lend any clues as to why he was seeking prayer at the alter. I have never had the Holy Spirit so strongly direct me in my life. He told me to go relay a message to this boy. As I stand in my pew I almost inwardly argue with the Holy Spirit saying I don't know this boy, he is obviously waiting for a pastor for prayer or help, I am no one, I am new here, I don't know how this works the pastor can help him. I almost immediately got nauseous at the thought of letting this boy go without being obedient to the Holy Spirit. I have NEVER had that feeling so strong in my life and it will honestly make non-believers want to send you on a one -way trip to the Looney bin if you describe the Spirit inside you directing you to speak to a random stranger.

My life experience up until this point has taught me always do what you are asked to do when you are asked to do it. So as I walked up to this boy in front of our entire church, I had no idea what to say, I almost panicked and then I got near him and I tapped him on the shoulder. I said whatever came out of my mouth. I didn't plan it, I don't know why I said what I did but I told him, "I have never had this happen to me before in my life and God has never spoken or commanded me this strongly but He wanted me to tell you that you deserve to feel the love He has for you and He loves you so much, you are important." As I started to walk away tears in my eyes and completely and utterly drained from the emotional roller coaster that just took place he grabbed my shoulder, shook his head and said with eyes filling with tears, "what did he tell you to say to me?" I repeated and then I added without a single bit of hesitation, "you cannot give up. It isn't the end for you, God loves you more than you will ever know, you cannot give up!" And then I felt instantly overwhelmed as if God had shown me what this boy was struggling with, he wanted to end it. I hugged him and told him how valuable he is and God is never going to let go of him and how much God loves him. He pulled away while still holding my shoulders on both sides and through tears he said thank you and started talking about feasting in heaven together. Everything in my body was so forcibly telling him not to give up. I don't even know this kid! We are at the front of my church, I'm crying and commanding this kid, whom I have no evidence of what the Spirit has led me to believe to feel Gods love and not give up.

The elders of the church must have recognized or sensed this boy's pain and immediately swooped in to begin praying and helping him as I slowly walked away exhausted and tears streaming. I had always been on the receiving end of powerful messages like that. While laying everything down on the alter the pastor would come up and speak a word from God that the pastor would have no way of knowing exactly what you are dealing with. I know that they have the ability to be used by God in that way but I really didn't think me, ordinary little me would ever do that. Yet, here I sit on July 19, as an insignificant one that God chose to use to hopefully save that young man's life. I cannot explain to you what that moment has done or how God has used that moment to help me to share this insight with you. You are MORE than just one. You are part of the POWERFUL MANY. It doesn't matter where you are in life, young, old, divorced, widowed, happy, sad, broke or rich, once you give your life to God and accept Christ as your savior you are one of His elite that He can use as the powerful one to save many. God can equip us with any strength, gift or achievement He so desires to help you accomplish the mission or task He lays before you and me.

The attitude or belief that we are just one comes from the enemy, when we are saved we ban together as the many that

God can use to save more lives and bring more people to see His glory. I often think of the disciples, your average men that just look the leap of faith to follow this man named Jesus, and yet their faith grew and multiplied and once Jesus was resurrected and the disciples were washed in the Holy Spirit they became powerhouses for God. They saved lives, built churches, banished demons, restored faith, and healed in the name of Jesus. These seemingly ordinary men, when saved and banned together by the Holy Spirit literally changed the course of history.

I think sometimes we make the mistake of seeing ourselves as insignificant so we can use it as a scapegoat to escape any real commitment we might have to make to Gods work. "Who am I to be a pastor? Who am I to start a Bible study? Who am I to save that person? Who am I to start that project?" Ever said any of these phrases and now are feeling super guilty about it? Just kidding, that is definitely not my intention. God doesn't work off the basis of work for guilt; he works on the premise of glory from blessings. Well I can honestly say I can write all those thoughts down so easily because I have had several of those myself or have heard others say exactly that. You are the one to do those things because you have been called to do them and you are not alone. You are never alone in anything God asks you to take on after you've been saved. You aren't alone when your mortgage is due and you have a family to feed and no income, you aren't alone when your husband leaves you after 30 years of marriage alone and confused, you aren't alone when the perfectly healthy pregnancy takes and awful turn and you lose the blessing you had been waiting forever for. God is with you through it all and you are one of the many. Many of us have felt your pain and do so on a regular basis and God is with you through it all, in the trenches with you working on turning all of our valleys into the highest peaks of our lives.

Once we adopt the understanding that we are never alone, that we are a powerful many that belong to the most high God, saved by grace and loved beyond measure we can start to see how God really does operated to help us personally but to use us to help one another. It is so amazing to see Him working in us helps to build the many and that one seemingly insignificant soul to our eyes can be so greatly held by God and used to a magnitude that we couldn't even dream of. If you're anything like me you can never picture yourself as one of those people God is going to use in such a grand scheme as part of the many but try this exercise. Really think about the people in your life and I bet you can name at least a few where you have seen God truly transform a seemingly lowly little one into a powerhouse for the Lord. He is working that same work in you. You are important, you are loved and you are powerful in the name of Jesus.

Together, when we recognize the power we have in the name of Jesus and in the love of our God we can accomplish anything He lays out before us. You are one, together we are many, and with God we are strong. Recognize the work He is doing around you in others and how to uses people in our lives to work for you personally and help others and you will see the glory God deserves for using His powerful many to save souls and change lives every day, you are one of those many. Be used, open up to the possibility of greatness in God and let yourself know that you are important and God has such amazing plans for your life. I constantly have to remind myself of this every day and sometimes multiple times a day but it is true and the more I remind myself the more I am lifted out of the pit and I start to avoid the situations, relationships and moments that brought me to the pit to begin with because I can see that God would not want those moments for my life, I am important and I am here to bring Him glory not be ashamed, in despair, hopeless, lost and alone. That is NOT His plan for me or you. If you feel like you are in that place, tell yourself you are NEVER alone, you are not just one you are one of the powerful many that God is holding so close to His breast and using to save so many others that feel exactly the way you do.

If you get anything out this chapter, take it back to the greatest commandment we can follow is to love our God above all and to love our neighbor as ourselves. I know it seems out of context but what any of this has taught me is to recognize that I am one of many but the many are ones too that have felt at some point lost and alone like I did and were rescued by the same Savior and how many more people in your life that you encounter on a daily basis are feeling that way? Love with all your heart and show mercy and compassion on others because life has taught me circumstances may be different but at the core all of us are caring some kind of pain that is shaping that person and you are one of the powerful many that can save those people. Do not feel like since you are not a "called pastor or preacher" that you aren't worthy to speak the word or breathe life into someone. God will equip you with the gift you need at the moment to be powerful in His name and do His will and work. I am so thankful God has taken me on this journey and I hope as I said, that if it could touch one life and give God the glory he deserves for saving mine then it was successful.

And I pray:

"God please let me continue to see my worth in your eyes. Please bless the many that will read this so they can see their worth and know that you don't see them as an insignificant one but as a powerful many that you love and will equip to not only successfully navigate their life personally but to make an impact in the lives of everyone around them. Please bless us with peace and comfort as we travel in those valleys and give us the strength to rest in your word and your promises to us that you are using all things for our good. Thank you for all

the good works you do in us, and thank you for all the people that you send us in our lives to help us to continue to grow in you. God we are praising you through the peaks but more importantly through the valleys because we know now that we are not an insignificant one but a powerful many that you love beyond compare. Thank you God. In Jesus name I pray Amen."

Samantha Gustafson is available for speaking engagements and public appearances. For more information contact:

Samantha Gustafson
C/O Advantage Books
P.O. Box 160847
Altamonte Springs, FL 32716

info@advbooks.com

To purchase additional copies of this book visit our online bookstore at: www.advbookstore.com

Longwood, Florida, USA
"we bring dreams to life"™
www.advbookstore.com

CPSIA information can be obtained
at www.ICGtesting.com
Printed in the USA
LVOW04s0239151215
466654LV00017B/192/P